The Three Tasks of Leadership

Worldly Wisdom for Pastoral Leaders

Edited by

Eric O. Jacobsen

William B. Eerdmans Publishing Company
Grand Rapids, Michigan / Cambridge, U.K.

Published 2009 by
Wm. B. Eerdmans Publishing Co.
2140 Oak Industrial Drive N.E., Grand Rapids, Michigan 49505 /
P.O. Box 163, Cambridge CB3 9PU U.K.

Printed in the United States of America

14 13 12 11 10 09   7 6 5 4 3 2 1

Library of Congress Cataloging-in-Publication Data

The three tasks of leadership: worldly wisdom for pastoral leaders /
edited by Eric O. Jacobsen.
p. cm.
Includes bibliographical references.
ISBN 978-0-8028-6398-0 (pbk.: alk. paper)
1. Pastoral theology. 2. Christian leadership. 3. Leadership — Religious aspects — Christianity. 4. Leadership. I. Jacobsen, Eric O.

BV4011.3.T48 2009
253 — dc22

2008043909

www.eerdmans.com

To Max De Pree

a leader of leaders

a teacher of teachers

Contents

Foreword

Beyond being a preacher and a pastor, the minister is also called to be a leader — a leader in his or her congregation, in broader church contexts, in the local community beyond the church, and sometimes even well beyond the local community. But what qualities are necessary for Christian ministerial leadership, both within the church and without? What are the essential tasks of it? What are the deepest principles that should inform such leadership? What important virtues should characterize the Christian leader in the pastorate? In which particular situations must the pastor demonstrate leadership, and through which particular modes does he or she do so?

This is a book about leadership meant both for pastors and for those still training to be pastors. The hope, then, is that it will be a useful guide for pastors already in congregations and also a useful text for seminary courses teaching prospective pastors about leadership. It addresses certain leadership issues that are directly relevant to the running of churches and other ecclesial structures. But it is also meant to help pastors as they preach and provide spiritual direction to people in their congregations, people who themselves may be called to lead in a variety of ways. The church and the world are in need of good, not just effective, leaders.

For wisdom in these matters, this book turns to one of the most respected and creative Christian leaders in the business community. Max De Pree was for many years the chairman and CEO of Herman Miller, Inc., a company known not only for innovative excellence in furniture design and manufacture, but also, thanks in large part to Max himself, for its creative and wise approach to corporate management and leadership. Max has also expressed his vision of leadership in a number of acclaimed and highly influential books on leadership, including the best-selling *Leadership Is an Art, Leadership Jazz,* and *Called to Serve.*

The occasion for the present book, which draws on Max's vision and insights, is his retirement from the Board of Trustees at Fuller Seminary in 2005. We at Fuller have wanted to do something to honor Max and recognize the profound influence he has had on the lives of leaders in a wide variety of fields. As members of an academic community, our first thought was to commission a Festschrift. However, we were prevented from going in this direction by a characteristic of Max himself that we deeply admire. One of the things we have most appreciated about Max's writing is his ability to express profound truths in an accessible manner. One doesn't have to be an expert to grasp the insights Max draws from his vast experience in management. This rare combination of depth and accessibility is one of the reasons that Max's writings have been so popular.

While Festschrifts are a common way for academics to confer honor on a particular individual, they tend to be neither accessible nor particularly popular. We decided, then, to ask our authors to write for an educated audience, but not "for the guild." That is to say, we asked them to minimize technical jargon and to keep the essays relatively short. We also decided to allow authors to work in areas they were passionate about, but to subject their essays to a somewhat rigorous organizational scheme so that each section could develop around a single theme. This organizational scheme derives from Max De Pree himself, and these parameters have allowed the final form of this project to have, we hope, the kind of coherence that will serve both classroom student and pastor well.

The other consideration we had to wrestle with was the apparent provincialism of the project. Most of the authors of these chapters are in some way connected to Fuller Theological Seminary. And while Fuller is one of the more diverse and multifaceted theological institutions, one could certainly envision an even broader scope of perspectives if we had chosen authors with no association with Fuller. However, this ties into another aspect of Max's work that we admire. Rather than try to feign mastery of global management practices in the abstract, Max found a seemingly inexhaustible font of wisdom in reflecting on his years of faithful experience at one company. Max wrote what he knew from Zeeland, Michigan, and people from all over the world have been blessed by it. Similarly we write from our particular setting at Fuller, believing that this specificity may in some ways enrich the book rather than diminish it.

This is all to say that this book has been inspired by Max De Pree, but it is not about Max De Pree. It represents insights mostly cultivated in the soil of Fuller Seminary but which are hoped to be helpful and relevant even to people who have never heard of Fuller Seminary. And what better way to honor someone than to produce a book that beyond simply paying tribute to the honoree, further extends the legacy by being genuinely helpful to others? We hope that for pastors and seminary students alike — and more broadly for all who must lead in the church — this will be such a book.

ERIC O. JACOBSEN

Introduction: Mentor to Mentor

Walt Wright

Editor's Introduction Max De Pree famously defined leadership in terms of three tasks: defining reality, saying thank you, and servanthood. He worked out this unique definition in the context of forty years at Herman Miller, Inc. This definition of leadership and the way De Pree develops it and applies it in his context are saturated with theologically informed wisdom. But it is wisdom that has been developed and tested in the boardroom rather than in the pulpit. What are the possibilities and limitations of taking De Pree's insights into a pastoral setting? In this essay Walt Wright, president of the De Pree Leadership Center and longtime mentee of Max De Pree, answers just that question.

Max De Pree's most quoted statement is his response to the question: What is leadership? "The first responsibility of a leader," he claims, "is to define reality. The last is to say thank you. In between the two, the leader must become a servant and a debtor."[1] This, of course, surfaces several questions: What is leadership? What are the responsibilities of leadership? What does it mean to define reality? Is there more to saying thank you than saying the words? What does it mean to serve and to owe?

1. Max De Pree, *Leadership Is an Art* (East Lansing: Michigan State University Press, 1987), 11.

What Is Leadership?

Leadership is once again a prominent theme in our culture. Most college and seminary catalogues announce an intention to produce leaders for society and church at a time when corporate leaders have replaced televangelists as the poster children of abuse of power and churches are removing pastors for leadership failures.[2] Government leaders watch as events spin out of control and declining approval ratings reduce their potential to lead. Leaders are critiqued for the abuse of power, for failure to deliver on promises, for inability to resolve conflict, and for uninspired vision. At the same time, the media calls for leaders who will show us the way forward and help us understand how to walk this journey of life.[3] Some look for questions to guide us in framing answers; others look for answers to diminish the risk of choice. Could it be that we focus too much on leaders and not enough on leadership?

Could it be that we focus too much on leaders and not enough on leadership?

Theories of leadership have tried to isolate the characteristics of great leaders. From great person theory to leadership traits, to personal charisma or intellect, to the need for power, researchers have tried to locate leadership in the person of the leader.[4] No single leader theory has won the day. Contingency theory seeks to explain leaders by their response to the immediate situation and the needs of the person they wish to influence.[5] More recent theories stress the relational nature of leadership, the dyadic link between leader and follower; or, to use a metaphor from the world of mountain climbing, leaders and followers are tied together. The rope, the relationship that connects them, is the locus of

2. A Midwest denominational leader told me recently that this year six of his pastors were fired by their churches for leadership failures. In no case was it an issue of preaching, theology, ecclesiology, or ethics. In every case it was inability to exercise leadership, to nurture relationships, to manage conflict, or to inspire vision.

3. Don Moyer, "Follow the Leader," *Harvard Business Review,* May 2006, 160.

4. Ronald Heifetz, *Leadership without Easy Answers* (Cambridge: Harvard University Press, 1994), 16-17. See also Gary Yukl, *Leadership in Organizations* (Englewood Cliffs, N.J.: Prentice-Hall, 1981), 1-9.

5. Paul Hersey and Kenneth Blanchard, *The Management of Organizational Behavior,* 5th ed. (Englewood Cliffs, N.J.: Prentice-Hall, 1988), 116.

leadership.[6] The advantage of this theory, which seems to be emerging as the dominant definition of leadership, is that it takes the focus off the leader and places it on the relationship. Leadership is a relationship of influence.[7]

Once leadership is defined as a relationship of influence, it is evident that everyone exercises leadership; we all seek to influence the people and circumstances around us. The burden of leadership no longer rests on the shoulders of the leader. It is shared responsibility in which everyone participates.[8] Organizations — churches — may grant us the responsibility to lead, may hold us accountable for mission and outcomes, but they do not eliminate the leadership influence of those to whom we are roped. Leaders — pastors — may be responsible, but everyone exercises leadership. As a pastor, you have a unique pulpit from which to influence the members of your congregation. Every week they gather to listen to your vision for the church, to see your relationship with God, and to hear your word from God for them. Every week you have the opportunity to renew the relationship one-on-one that you have with each man and woman sitting in the pews. Yet, as you know so well, your relationship with each member also influences your vision for the church and the emphasis of your sermons. And your relationship with the governing bodies influences the strategies you select and the vision you implement. *Leadership is a relationship of influence in which one person seeks to influence the vision, the values, the attitudes, and the behaviors of another.* The church expects you to exercise leadership as its pastor. You know that the people exercise leadership when they choose to follow.

And that is another important piece of the definition. Leadership is about choice. That is one of the things I learned from Max De Pree. Leadership is more about following than leading. Until someone chooses to accept your influence, you have not led. In many ways leadership rests in the hands of the followers. They must choose to respond to your influence and act before leadership has occurred. That is why the mountaineering rope metaphor is so powerful. If leaders and followers are tied into

6. Walter Wright, *Don't Step on the Rope! Reflections on Leadership, Relationships, and Teamwork* (Colorado Springs: Authentic Paternoster, 2005).

7. James M. Kouzes and Barry Z. Posner, *Credibility: How Leaders Gain and Lose It, Why People Demand It* (San Francisco: Jossey-Bass, 1993), 1.

8. James M. Kouzes and Barry Z. Posner, *The Leadership Challenge*, 3rd ed. (San Francisco: Jossey-Bass, 2002), 27.

the same rope, no one moves unless everyone chooses to move. And the leader will move in the direction that the followers choose to move regardless of title. Leadership is a relationship of influence.

Pastors influence through words and behaviors. Your congregation listens to your words and watches your behavior. And they choose which one to follow. In their choice you have exercised leadership. Which, of course, is why integrity becomes so important. Integrity is the alignment of word and behavior — doing what you say is important. When leaders lack integrity, followers may choose to follow behavior instead of advice. Leadership is still exercised, just not as intended. Leadership is a relationship of influence as perceived by and acted on by the followers.

My grandson Brendon is six years old. He has no title, no positional authority, but he has immense power to influence my behavior. Through the loving relationship of grandparent and grandchild he regularly exercises leadership, influencing what I do and say. Last summer he illustrated brilliantly the reality that leadership is a relationship of influence, not a position or a person.

Brendon's father, my son, lives north of San Francisco and has a guesthouse on his property in Marin County. Last summer the CEO of a company in San Francisco and his wife and daughter stayed in the guesthouse for several weeks while their own home was being remodeled. During this time they took a vacation to Hawaii. The CEO asked my grandson Brendon, then five years old, if he would feed the cat while they were in Hawaii. The CEO offered ten cents per day. Brendon thought for a moment and responded, "No. That is not enough for me to have to remember it every day." The CEO countered with: "Okay, I'll give you twenty-five cents a day." Brendon replied, "No. That is still not enough to have to do it every day." So the CEO asked how much Brendon wanted. Brendon suggested one dollar per day, and negotiations began. They settled on fifty cents per day to feed the cat while the CEO's family was on vacation.

On the morning of their trip, the CEO took Brendon out to the guesthouse, showed him the cat food and the bowls and restated the agreement: "You will feed the cat every morning and I will give you fifty cents per day. Is that clear?" Brendon looked up at him with large blue eyes and asked innocently, "Did you want water also?" . . . That was another fifty cents per day!

Position, authority, age, and charisma are not the determiners of leadership. Leadership is exercised whenever one person influences the vision, values, attitudes, or behaviors of another and the other person chooses to act. Leadership is dependent upon the choice to follow, whether a CEO or a five-year-old.

What Are the Responsibilities of Leadership?

Leadership is responsible to articulate the mission, reinforce the culture, empower the people, and say thank you. Max De Pree talks about defining reality. That includes keeping the vision and values prominent in the community. Max speaks of becoming a servant and a debtor. Service finds expression in releasing the potential in people, helping them see how their work contributes to the larger mission of the community. The debt is paid by providing the resources, space, delegation, encouragement, and accountability they need to succeed. And borrowing directly from Max, I see in the expression of thanks a profound reframing of the leader's reality. Leaders are dependent upon followers for the exercise of leadership and the accomplishment of mission. Max has captured well the heart of leadership: defining reality, saying thank you, and serving people and mission.

What Does It Mean to Define Reality?

Leaders define reality with words, actions, and questions. With words we keep the purpose, the mission, the vision before the community. With our actions we teach that what we believe is important, and over time our values take root in the culture of the community. With questions we encourage others to own the present and participate in creating the future.

Every Sunday morning you stand before your people and define reality. The unique power of the pulpit proclaiming the Word of God frames the reality in which you and your congregation are living. You are remembering the theological story that enfolds your com-

The way you relate to the church secretary, the way you treat the man from the street, the way you react to the reporter who calls, the way you treat the gardener and the many volunteers that surround your ministry reveal what is truly important to you.

munity; you are articulating the vision that defines the unique mission of your church in your city. You are helping the people who look to you for leadership reflect theologically on their daily lives, their Christian calling, and their eternal hope. In your sermons, your teaching, your writing, and your memos you are teaching theology to the people who expect you to lead them in this area of their lives. Every leader in every organization is responsible to keep the mission alive, but few have the pulpit available to pastors. If power is the potential and the opportunity to influence people, then pastors have been given an incredible power base. Use it wisely; it is a gift from God.

But your most powerful teaching does not emanate from the pulpit. It occurs in the living of your life, in the conduct of your work, and in your relationships with your people. Current research in emotional intelligence is underlining what you have known for a long time. The primary influence of the leadership relationship occurs more strongly at the emotional level than at the intellectual level. In fact, the emotional connection between people is twice as powerful as intellect, knowledge, or competence when it comes to influencing others.[9] Parishioners attend your services, they hear your words, but they listen to the heart they have encountered as they engage you in life. You teach more when you visit people at their work, in their homes, in their crises, and in their celebrations than you do in your sermons. Or perhaps more accurately, it is the relational encounters with the people that open them to hear the word God speaks through you on Sunday. And it goes deeper than this. The way you relate to the church secretary, the way you treat the man from the street, the way you react to the reporter who calls, the way you treat the gardener and the many volunteers that surround your ministry reveal what is truly important to you. As Max De Pree articulates so eloquently, we teach what is important in every action we perform. Our character is communicated in the values revealed in our behaviors.[10] In the everyday actions of life and work, in the decisions that accrue daily, you are teaching what you really believe, and as pastor — a person called to shepherd

9. Daniel Goleman, *Working with Emotional Intelligence* (New York: Bantam Books, 1998), 320.

10. Daniel Goleman, Richard Boyatzis, and Annie McKee, *Primal Leadership: Realizing the Power of Emotional Intelligence* (Boston: Harvard Business School Press, 2002), 121-22.

or lead and love the congregation — you are defining the reality that will influence people's walk before God. This is a sobering reality.

Everything we do teaches that what we believe is important. That is why you and I and Max take mentoring so seriously. Mentors come alongside and ask the questions about who we intend to be, how our actions and sermons align, or as Max would say, how our voice and touch connect.[11] Mentors are the question askers on our journey, the men and women who rope to us to provide a belay — a relationship that holds us when we stumble and assists us in learning from our falls. We have long known the value of mentors to those they mentor. But in addition, recent research in affective neuroscience and biology suggests that mentoring in caring, compassionate relationships does something in the brain of the mentor that offsets the impact of power stress resulting from leadership responsibility.[12] So these mentoring relationships we have encouraged are health-giving to both mentor and mentee. But then we know that from experience. The asking of reality-framing questions because we want a person to realize his or her potential is a learning time for leaders and followers.

Max De Pree has long advocated the power of the apropos question to frame the reality in which we find ourselves. In doing so he draws on biblical wisdom. Jesus used stories and questions to open the minds of his hearers to larger horizons of thinking. "Who do you say that I am?" (Mark 8:29) elicits a behavior-shaping response from Peter, as does the poignant repetition of "Do you love me?" (John 21:15-17). By word and by action he had been teaching the disciples about the kingdom of God. Yet the sowing of a question allows an answer to take root in the hearts and minds of his followers that shapes their lives and their leadership. The power of question and choice is revealed early in Scripture. In the creation narrative, Adam is placed in the garden and allowed to name the living creatures presented by the Creator (Gen. 2:19). The text does not elaborate yet leaves a picture less of choosing a name (from among alternatives) than of pronouncing a name in God-like fashion. Choice occurs later with a question from the serpent. The first recorded question in the

11. Max De Pree, *Leadership Jazz* (New York: Currency Doubleday, 1992), 3.

12. Richard E. Boyatzis, Melvin L. Smith, and Nancy Blaize, "Developing Sustainable Leaders through Coaching and Compassion," *Academy of Management Learning and Education* 5, no. 1 (2006): 12.

Bible becomes "Did God really say . . . ?" (Gen. 3:1). With that subtle question choice enters the garden and humankind is forever seduced. Behavior can be influenced. And it is God who defines the new reality with another question: "Adam, where are you?" (Gen. 3:9). Did the Creator really need to be told where Adam was? Or did Adam need to take responsibility for his choice? God's question and Adam's answer define the new reality and all the behaviors that flow from it. Questions create choice and choice expects ownership. As management consultant Peter Block says, "Getting the question right may be the most important thing we can do. We define our dialogue and, in a sense, our future through the questions we choose to address."[13]

People look to leaders, to the men and women whose influence they value, to define reality. Through words that keep us focused on what matters, through behaviors that teach what is important, and through questions that require commitment, leaders frame the reality in which we choose the paths to walk. Here are a few questions for you to consider:

- Where do you see God at work?
- Where do your people see God at work?
- How does your preaching frame the reality of people's marketplace experience?
- What theology of vocation are you teaching?
- When your daughters follow you around, what are they learning about God?
- What is the measure of success in Christian ministry? In Christian life?
- What do you expect from God?
- What does God expect from you?

Your answers will begin to define the reality you are framing.

13. Peter Block, *The Answer to How Is Yes: Acting on What Matters* (San Francisco: Berrett-Koehler, 2002), 13.

Is There More to Saying Thank You Than Saying the Words?

Kouzes and Posner in the classic text *The Leadership Challenge* argue that saying thank you is a concrete way of showing respect and strengthening the relationship between leaders and followers.[14] I think it is more than that. Saying thank you is an acknowledgment of dependence. As I noted above, leaders and followers are roped together; they are interdependent. There is no leadership without followers. There is no influence without choice and commitment. And leadership — influence — flows both ways in the leadership relationship. Saying thank you is a visible, public declaration of dependence. It presupposes an attitude of humility, an appropriate valuing of each person's contribution. I think that is what Paul is getting at in Romans 12. I have always appreciated that while leadership (προϊστάμενος) is included as one of the gifts Paul identifies within the church, it is not first or last. It is sandwiched between giving money and helping people. Which encourages me to paraphrase Romans 12:3 for Christian leaders: "Don't take yourself too seriously!" Leadership exists to some extent only to create space for other gifts to be released. It has no priority of importance and finds its success in the accomplishment of others. "Thank you" is a statement that defines reality for the leader.

So how do you say thank you? Foundationally we need to remember to say it — often — for our own benefit as much as for those we acknowledge. Say it in person; say it in writing. And it also can be built into our community relationships: celebrating accomplishments, appreciating failures, acknowledging growth. Organizationally I believe churches, like any other gathering of people with purpose, should take performance reviews and feedback seriously. Performance reviews are the structural way that organizations create opportunity to say thank you, to acknowledge interdependence, and to encourage growth. Thank you is the flip side of accountability. Performance reviews, when done well, communicate respect, value, and partnership to those we seek to lead in the church. And you know that I

Performance reviews are the structural way that organizations create opportunity to say thank you.

14. Kouzes and Posner, *The Leadership Challenge,* 368.

believe everyone — paid staff and volunteers — deserves feedback, accountability, and recognition. When leaders do not make the investment in performance reviews, they communicate that the contribution is not significant. Of course, a well-conducted performance review also seeks feedback and accountability for the leader.[15] Leaders and followers are tied together; they are interdependent. They owe one another this vulnerability and encouragement. More questions to ponder:

- Who is on your rope?
- Who did you thank today?
- How do you express respect and appreciation?
- What is the relationship of gratitude and accountability?
- How seriously do you take performance reviews?
- In performance reviews, are people encouraged or graded?
- How do you celebrate contribution?
- How do you appreciate failure?
- What does it mean to be dependable?

What Does It Mean to Serve and to Owe?

I like the way Max uses the process verb "to become." "In between . . . the leader must become a servant and a debtor." Leadership is learned as we engage one another. Defining reality and acknowledging dependence frame the leadership relationship, but serving and owing define it.

The idea of leader as servant has roots in Scripture (Mark 10:42-45; 1 Kings 12:7) but finds popular expression in the writing of Robert Greenleaf. Drawing on his Quaker heritage, Greenleaf approached leadership in corporation, academy, and church as the work of a servant.[16] The posture of servant acknowledges immediately that leaders serve something or someone greater than themselves. In all organizations we would argue that leaders first serve the gods they follow, then the mission that brings them and their followers into relationship, and finally the followers

15. For a suggested model for performance reviews, see Walter C. Wright, *Relational Leadership* (Carlisle, England: Paternoster, 2000), 170-79.

16. Robert K. Greenleaf, *Servant Leadership: A Journey into the Nature of Legitimate Power and Greatness* (New York: Paulist, 1977).

whose work achieves the mission. In the church this is made explicit in your ordination. You are called to the ministry of Word and sacrament in the name of Jesus to serve the congregation that embraces your call. Pastors stand in the pulpit as the anointed leader of the community, but first as a follower of Jesus Christ. You exercise leadership, but you are not the leader. God is the leader. When kings, shepherds, pastors, or executives forget that, they put at risk all who follow them.

Leadership exists within organizations, including the church, to polish gifts, create community, and focus energy on the shared mission, the reason for gathering. When we organize for a purpose, that purpose becomes the measure of organizational activity. Even in the church, where organization and community compete for attention, the answer to the question, What would be lost if we went out of business? is the purpose that followers, members of the congregation, expect leadership to serve. Leadership broadly understood is a relationship of influence. Within the structure of church and organization leadership is expected to serve the mission that defines the community. Service finds expression in releasing the potential in people, helping them see how their work contributes to the larger mission of the community. Service is about God, mission, and people.

Leaders first serve the gods they follow, then the mission that brings them and their followers into relationship, and finally the followers whose work achieves the mission.

Leadership serves the God that the leader follows. It serves the mission that creates the organizational relationship of leader and follower. But also, leadership serves the people who choose to follow. This is how leaders become servants and debtors. Debt is paid by providing the resources, space, delegation, encouragement, and accountability people need to succeed. Leaders owe those who choose to follow:

- space to become the persons they can be — choice to become the persons they intend to be — possibility to release their potential.
- the opportunity to serve, to make a contribution, to be needed.
- challenges and constraints that unleash creativity.
- encouragement to risk learning and liberty to fail.
- freedom to change.

- opportunity to make a commitment and be accountable — to have purpose and meaning.
- delegation and responsibility — the power to choose and influence outcomes — to lead.
- clarity of mission, expectations, and the possibility for growth.
- a place to belong, defined by intimacy, vulnerability, interdependence, and involvement.[17]

This list raises many questions to ponder, but they can be summed up in three fundamental questions for leadership:

- Whom do you serve?
- How have the men and women who choose to follow your leadership grown?
- At the end of your life, what will be the legacy of your leadership?

Two passages from the Old Testament always loom in my mind when I reflect on these questions.

The first is 2 Chronicles 21:20: "Jehoram was thirty-two years old when he became king, and he reigned in Jerusalem eight years. He passed away, to no one's regret, and was buried in the City of David, but not in the tombs of the kings." He passed away to no one's regret! What a sad epitaph. He took his eyes off of God in whose service he led. And his leadership led his people astray — a frightening legacy.

The second is the last words of David:

The oracle of David son of Jesse,
  the oracle of the man exalted by the Most High,
the man anointed by the God of Jacob,
  Israel's singer of songs.
The Spirit of the LORD spoke through me;
  his word was on my tongue.
The God of Israel spoke,
  the Rock of Israel said to me:
"When one rules over people in righteousness,
  when one rules in the fear of God,

17. Many of these debts are listed in De Pree, *Leadership Is an Art,* 35-40, 64-65.

that one is like the light of morning at sunrise
  on a cloudless morning,
like the brightness after rain
  that brings the grass from the earth."
Is not my house right with God?
  Has God not made with me an everlasting covenant,
  arranged and secured in every part?
Will God not bring to fruition my salvation
  and grant me my every desire?

(2 Sam. 23:1-5)

Shepherd, singer, slayer of giants, brigand, mercenary, king, and murderer — David is the Old Testament prototype for leadership that follows after God. Placed in his position by God, David stumbled visibly but continued to lead as a servant of God. At the end of his life he could look back on his wild journey and celebrate that God indeed spoke through his leadership — that people grew and thrived under his leadership on behalf of God. Repeating the image of Psalm 72, he likens leadership to the rain and the sun that brings new growth to the garden. That is a legacy for leadership: God is served and people thrive.

With appropriate humility may you continue to lead your church as a servant of God. With integrity of word and action may you define a reality that releases the spirit of your people. May your life and leadership proclaim praise and gratitude to the God you follow and the people you serve.

TASK 1 Defining Reality

1 Leadership as Interpreting Reality

Marguerite Shuster

Editor's Introduction One of the concerns for pastors in borrowing wisdom from the world of business is that this world seems so very different from the world of the church. To those on the outside, the corporate world seems to be one of leveraging power and rewarding achievement while the world of the church seems to be about mutual submission and reliance upon grace. In this essay Marguerite Shuster, who teaches theology and preaching at Fuller Seminary, takes a hard look at defining reality to discern whether it really has a legitimate role in the church. While expressing caution about applying this maxim sloppily, she ultimately shows that so long as defining reality can be employed with a healthy doctrine of human sinfulness, it can be a wonderful channel of grace both in the world of business and in the church.

Among the fundamental tasks for leaders considered in this volume, perhaps no single one has been more readily and eagerly embraced than the responsibility to "define reality" — indeed, that responsibility gives the title to the first section of the book. On the face of it, it is a heady, even intoxicating, idea. Of course, it might mean nothing more than the quite modest observation, commonplace in postmodern culture, that a set of circumstances must be interpreted, and will inevitably be interpreted, before we can respond to it appropriately or even at all. Are we looking at a bank robbery or a movie shoot? Is

> **A set of circumstances must be interpreted, and will inevitably be interpreted, before we can respond to it appropriately or even at all.**

the business opening down the street a threatening competitor or a potential customer? Should we regard the new theological development as a breath of fresh air that will strengthen the faithful, or as the thread that when pulled will unravel the whole fabric of the faith once delivered to the saints? No leader of an organization directly concerned with any such matter can afford to let the rule for construal be "every person for himself or herself." Of course a leader must take a position, must "define reality." On the other hand, in the hands of the unprincipled, insecure, or power hungry, the rubric could be taken to imply the leader's right to say to his or her followers, "my way or the highway," to "tell them how it is." Those who react with a visceral twinge of anxiety to unnuanced affirmation of this fundamental role of a leader may fear its arrogant and self-interested application.

Let us suppose, however, that we intend to speak of the ordinary leader who is not megalomaniacal, but whose visionary responsibilities go beyond flat-footed discrimination of bank robberies from movie shoots. This leader must make choices in situations where the facts can responsibly be viewed in very different ways. What I propose to affirm is that in situations of that sort, possibilities for "defining reality" open to a responsible leader are rightly constrained by underlying realities of a theological sort, realities that can be violated only at unacceptable cost. These realities limit equally the ends that may properly be envisioned and sought and the means that may properly be employed. They are not a sort of addition to be considered alongside sometimes competing responsibilities to, say, produce maximal return for shareholders; they rather determine whether, in the end, one will be judged to have built with wood, hay, and stubble, or with gold, silver, and precious stones (1 Cor. 3:12).

First and foremost, let us be clear that there is no right way to do the wrong thing. It is no virtue to have built well what should not have been built at all. The idea that there is really nothing we should not do at all had a bad beginning (Gen. 3:1) and will surely come to a bad end. Calvin and Luther were both adamant that one could cobble shoes to the glory of God — a secular vocation can be a holy one; but if you are manufacturing biological weapons, making the best ones is not a virtue, whether you are responsible for the overall strategy of the enterprise or spend your days sterilizing petri dishes. Nor ought a pastor to be plotting ways to get the best of a fellow pastor. A good deal of grief might be avoided if leaders began by asking straightforwardly whether what they are considering is something they can sincerely contemplate doing before God. (The difficulty of doing so honestly, given human pride and willfulness, is a matter we shall touch upon in due course.)

A good deal of grief might be avoided if leaders began by asking straightforwardly whether what they are considering is something they can sincerely contemplate doing before God.

Assuming the fundamental integrity of a leader's purposes, the next most basic matter is that leader's view of the persons with whom he or she works. At the risk of going against usage that has become almost universal, I would suggest that the very category "human resources" gets it exactly wrong from the very outset. It places people made in the image of God right alongside two-by-fours, power generators, and textbooks as material needed to get the job done: human beings become more or less useful instruments in service of reaching a particular end. Their worth is not intrinsic but relative to the goal at hand. It might be, of course, that leaders of a particular organization would protest that they do not "really" mean that in a grand ontological sense, but that they do, after all, have a job to do and must be both firm and discriminating in determining who can help get it done and who cannot. True, but there is all the difference in the world between a Donald Trump, with his trademark, and arrogant, "You're fired!" and a Max De Pree, who asks the underachieving worker if she can do better, or if she knows of another job in the company that would better fit her gifts, or if she would like some time to relocate.

It may be, of course, that the latter approach produces an atmosphere in which everyone in the organization does better work and produces better results in the long run. If so, that might be an example of what colleagues have dubbed "the moral nature of the universe."[1] Perhaps God has in fact set things up in such a way that at least sometimes, doing the right and good thing produces concrete earthly results. ("Honesty is the best policy.") But these results must not become the essential reason for the leadership practice. Not only does one not know ahead of time what the appropriate time frame might be for eval-

1. Nancey Murphy and George Ellis, *On the Moral Nature of the Universe: Theology, Cosmology, and Ethics* (Minneapolis: Fortress, 1996).

uating such results (there are no guarantees!), but discerning employees will smell it a mile off when they are being managed and manipulated by presumably humane and enlightened practices. Performing "the right act for the wrong reason" may be worse than acting in a straightforwardly self-interested way, for people will feel more betrayed by being deceived by someone they trusted than by being misused by someone they never trusted at all. Right acts cannot in the end be severed from right purposes.

To say that persons are important and must be treated as having intrinsic worth and dignity is not to say that work, and work of good quality, is not important. Much to the contrary. Work is not in itself a curse brought on by the fall, which we are simply to endure until we make it to retirement. Work is a creation ordinance (Gen. 2:15) without which human beings do not normally find fulfillment. The leader who seeks to help others find a meaningful place to contribute is working with the grain of the created order; and the leader who expects good work thereby treats the one who does it as a person of dignity. To proceed as if one should accept the sloppy, mindless, and careless is not to act kindly but to insult others.

At the same time, it takes a special knack, and a special humility, to recognize deeply that without faithful people in the less glamorous and less readily recognized posts, no organization can function. Good maintenance people are utterly indispensable. A splendid church secretary is about as hard to come by as a splendid pastor. All those sermons on 1 Corinthians 12 might sound less tiresome if we did better at actually believing them: not everyone is or should try to be a leader; and the truth that "too many cooks spoil the broth" should not be read to suggest that we should each get our own kitchen. Leaders who see clearly how dependent they are on a vast diversity of gifts are not being sentimental, but merely realistic.

All it takes for things to go seriously wrong is for a comparatively small number of people to "do what comes naturally."

If one truly believes this principle, then being intentional about offering a full range of opportunities to persons of both genders, all ethnic backgrounds, and various physical and intellectual strengths and limitations is not a matter of political correctness but one of recognizing what will be best in the long run for the organization as well as for the individuals involved.

The good is fragile. All it takes for things to go seriously wrong is for a comparatively small number of people to "do what comes naturally": to let self-interest and selfishness prevail; to slough off; to get jealous; to deceive themselves about their underlying motives; to blind themselves to the predictable harmful effects of their behavior on others; to neglect to notice assorted inconvenient truths. Of course, the more power and influence a person has in an organization, the more quickly such faults corrupt the whole. Therefore, a leader needs first of all to be alert to such temptations in himself or herself and — no doubt hardest of all — to have the humility to be open to input from those who can see readily enough from the outside what no sinful human sees easily from the inside. But he or she also needs to uproot quickly the seeds of these troubles wherever they begin to sprout, for an infection can rise up through the ranks as well. A robust understanding of the universality of human sinfulness can help a leader to see such matters as both ordinary and serious at the same time. They are ordinary in that they are, in large if not in detail, utterly predictable. If one sees nothing of them, one either is not looking or has sensibilities that are exceedingly poorly developed. They are serious in the way any virulent, death-dealing infection is serious. As sinners themselves, leaders are in a poor position to act either shocked or sanctimonious at manifestations of sin, but they must certainly move swiftly and firmly if destructive attitudes or behaviors seem to be taking hold. It would be delusional to suppose that one could weed out sin (and an uptight scrupulosity is no virtue), but one can contain many of its larger outward manifestations. Doing so matters.

As sinners themselves, leaders are in a poor position to act either shocked or sanctimonious at manifestations of sin, but they must certainly move swiftly and firmly if destructive attitudes or behaviors seem to be taking hold.

In organizations, matters are yet more complicated than they are with individuals or small groups. As Reinhold Niebuhr discerned in speaking of "moral man and immoral society," or as Walter Wink has more recently said in speaking of the "angels" or the pervasive spiritual ethos of institutions, states, companies, or churches: a character pervades organizations of all sorts that goes beyond the individuals that make them up.[2] Many will notice that in certain settings, new leaders come quickly to behave astonishingly like the leaders they replaced, and people do not seem to deliberately or unconsciously choose a new leader that is like the one they had before. Instead, at least some of the time, the very position itself seems to draw out certain character traits and not others, for good or ill. Something similar happens elsewhere in the organization, as people are shaped by a particular environment and culture. We speak of structural evil because these larger moods and tendencies are bigger than the individuals involved, and because it is easier for the influence to be negative than positive when individual responsibility and character are swallowed up by forces beyond individual control. Not only does one not *feel* as responsible for outcomes when they rest on the decisions of many others; one as a matter of fact often *cannot* change even what one sees as wrong. A sense of impotence generates passivity, and a downward spiral results. Not only do organizations thus tend to behave less morally than the individuals that make them up, but they sweep those individuals up into the immoral patterns of behavior; and such patterns are astonishingly hard to break. (I can recall, for example, a church that I observed manifesting a very destructive internal dynamic when I was a child; and now, more than forty years and more than half a dozen pastors later, it is still doing the same old destructive things.) The point, of course, is that good leaders need to use the greatest diligence to keep negative institutional patterns from getting started in the first place.[3]

But if the worst sorts of institutional fragility are due to sin, still, not all of them are. Many are simply due to finitude, which is not the same thing (although it may lead to sin precisely when people incline to deny their human limits). Some failures and mistakes come quite straightforwardly from greater or lesser degrees of weakness and ignorance — ordinary human lack of omnipotence, omniscience, omnipresence, and all those other competencies that belong to God alone. It is a very good

2. Reinhold Niebuhr, *Moral Man and Immoral Society* (New York: Scribner, 1948); Walter Wink, *Engaging the Powers: Discernment and Resistance in a World of Domination* (Minneapolis: Fortress, 1992).

3. One may note here the way in which the Scanlon Plan works against structural evil because each worker is placed in a position of responsibility for the whole. This factor may be as important theologically as it has been effective economically. (See, for instance, Max De Pree, *Leadership Is an Art* [New York: Doubleday, 1989], 97.)

thing if leaders keep in mind that they and their followers lack divine competence. If they do, they will make plenty of room for failure, which principle may be one of the most freeing of all assumptions about fellow workers. If people are gifted to be creative and to work at the limit of their knowledge and capacity, of course they will fail sometimes; if they don't, they are probably not being anywhere near adventurous enough. But a finite, limited human being is not free to be adventurous if her leader cannot tolerate failure.

In a safe and healthy organization, then, fragilities due to sin will be recognized both as evils that must be curbed and as faults that are the proper object of forgiveness, when the person involved can recognize and rue the fault and receive the grace of pardon. Fragilities due to finitude require not forgiveness but space and acceptance: they will seldom get out of hand except when sins (like pride or sloth or envy) creep in, or unless leaders lack the discernment to help people find positions that fit their gifts. These attitudes of forgiveness and acceptance, too, are manifestations of grace, grace that all of us require if we are to flourish and grow.

No theological principle is more central than our human need for grace.

In the end, then, no theological principle is more central than our human need for grace — God's saving grace first of all, but secondarily those manifestations of grace potentially reflected in every aspect of our daily lives. Only by keeping a firm grasp on grace can leaders even risk seeing accurately themselves and others, in all their potential and in all their frailty; for only thus are there resources for dealing with the surprising capacities and the surprising faults that can both appear as threats. And leaders who know deeply their own need for grace, who grant grace to others, and who seek forthrightly to do what they do before God, are in the best position to view reality — even before they seek to define it — in a way that honors the Lord.[4]

4. De Pree actually recommends putting the question within an organization, "What would grace enable us to be?" (*Leadership Jazz* [New York: Currency Doubleday, 1992], 83; *Leading without Power: Finding Hope in Serving Community* [San Francisco: Jossey-Bass, 1997], 55).

2 Defining the Reality of Your Role: Historical Contexts and Theological Models of Christian Leadership

Charles J. Scalise

Editor's Introduction During the last few decades we have become increasingly aware of the importance of metaphor in shaping our understanding of reality. Some claim that the metaphors we carry do more to shape our behavior than many of the ethical and normative rules we uphold. This situation challenges us to think much more carefully about which metaphors shape the reality of our pastoral identity. Where do they come from and how are they to be evaluated theologically? In this essay Charles Scalise, who teaches church history at Fuller Theological Seminary, examines the shepherd and CEO as primary metaphors for contemporary pastors. Rather than affirming one and rejecting the other, Scalise recommends that we understand the implications of our dominant metaphor but also be ready to employ different metaphors for different situations demanding leadership.

> *"We shall better keep our bearing among all the diversities and changes of this history if we remember that the word 'ministry' serves, not only to designate the full number of the church's leaders, but also to designate the true meaning of Christian leadership."*
>
> John Knox, "The Ministry in the Primitive Church"[1]

1. John Knox, "The Ministry in the Primitive Church," in *The Ministry in Historical*

I would like to express my thanks to my Fuller colleague David Augsburger, who extended an invitation to contribute this article, to editors Eric Jacobsen and Jon Pott, and especially to three pastors who took time from their busy schedules to read and offer suggestions for improvement: Judith Gay, Jane Maynard, and Don Schatz.

All Christians are called to the ministry of Christ in the world.[2] Among the varied gifts of the Spirit are special gifts for leadership[3] among the people of God. As Ephesians 4:11-12 observes, "The gifts he [Christ] gave were that some would be apostles, some prophets, some evangelists, some pastors and teachers *to equip the saints for the work of ministry.*"[4] The Christian church therefore has recognized among its membership the gifts for this equipping leadership, as God has called persons to vocations of Christian service.

Institutional calls to leadership in ministry reflect quite different levels of Christian life than personal calls of the Spirit.

The diverse processes of these ecclesiastical recognitions of vocation[5] are complex, tradition-laden, and often controversial. Contrasting the election of a pope to the call of a youth minister can provide some idea of this dramatic variety. Alternatively, one might simply ask almost any North American

---

Perspectives, ed. H. Richard Niebuhr and Daniel D. Williams (New York: Harper and Row, 1956), 1-26, at 2.

2. For a useful theological exposition of this theme, see Norman Pittenger, *The Ministry of All Christians: A Theology of Lay Ministry* (Wilton, Conn.: Morehouse-Barlow, 1983).

3. Max De Pree has written a number of lively, practical works on leadership and management (*Called to Serve: Creating and Nurturing the Effective Volunteer Board* [Grand Rapids: Eerdmans, 2001]; *Leadership Is an Art* [New York: Doubleday, 1989]; *Leadership Jazz* [New York: Currency Doubleday, 1992]; *Leading without Power: Finding Hope in Serving Community* [San Francisco: Jossey-Bass, 1997]). De Pree correlates his Christian faith with his practices of Christian leadership. He has not only described but also embodied this connection between faith and service in his life and work. (See Max De Pree, *Dear Zoe: Letters to My Grandchild on the Wonder of Life* [Grand Rapids: Eerdmans, 1996] for a personal portrait of his Christian faith in family life.) This investigation of the significance of historical contexts and theological models for analyzing images of Christian leadership is gratefully dedicated to him.

4. Unless otherwise noted, all English translations of biblical passages in this chapter follow the New Revised Standard Version (New York: Division of Christian Education of the National Council of Churches of Christ in the United States of America, 1989).

5. For more discussion of "the ecclesiastical call" as one of four elements of the call to ministry, see H. Richard Niebuhr, with Daniel Day Williams and James Gustafson, *The Purpose of the Church and Its Ministry* (New York: Harper and Row, 1956), 63-66.

seminary student seeking ordination in an old-line Protestant denomination to recount his or her experience of the process and its perplexing concatenations. Institutional calls to leadership in ministry reflect quite different levels of Christian life from personal calls of the Spirit.[6]

The puzzling diversity of patterns of Christian leadership can be attributed to the strikingly varied perspectives on the nature of ministry. These perspectives are dependent upon different understandings of the church that in turn are both formed and confirmed by diverse patterns of *images* in the Scripture. In the New Testament alone Paul Minear has catalogued ninety-six interrelated images of the church.[7] Besides familiar images like "the body of Christ" and "the people of God," the New Testament describes the church with lesser-known analogies like "the pillar and bulwark of the truth" (1 Tim. 3:15) and "the elect lady" (2 John 1). Given this biblical diversity, one should not be surprised by the proliferating models of ministry leadership visible in the church today.[8]

Pastors commonly report a sense of "whiplash," as they struggle to move rapidly from one set of demands to the next.

Busy pastors and other vocational church leaders regularly encounter diverse and often contradictory expectations of their identity as Christian leaders. Often these expectations lurk just beneath the surface of daily interactions. For instance, one moment a pastor is expected to interact primarily as a "chaplain," who serves the immediate needs of members of the congregation, while the next moment the pastor is expected to be a "visionary yet practical leader," who wisely guides the congregation into its future. Pastors commonly report a sense of "whiplash," as they struggle to move rapidly from one set of demands to the next.[9] One effective way to

6. For example, few seminarians who experience a call to pastoral ministry can realistically envision the challenge of holding their practice of spiritual disciplines together with the daily administrative demands of congregational life.

7. Paul Minear, *Images of the Church in the New Testament* (Philadelphia: Westminster, 1960).

8. For a recent review of a number of contemporary leadership models, see Robert Banks and Bernice M. Ledbetter, *Reviewing Leadership: A Christian Evaluation of Current Approaches* (Grand Rapids: Baker Academic, 2004).

9. Jane Maynard observes, "In my experience, [business and family] 'models' coexist uneasily in most congregations. Pastors . . . often tend to vacillate from one to an-

respond to these diverse expectations is to reflect critically upon the images that control them.

Our study will examine briefly two master images of the Christian leader that have attained prominence in the history of the Western church: the shepherd and the CEO[10] or, more broadly, the business executive.[11] We will then compare these two master images, utilizing three theological models for connecting theology and ministry, selected from five types I have analyzed in previous research.[12] The contrasting images of the shepherd and business executive will offer a practical illustration of the value of developing historical and theological perspective on contemporary studies of leadership in ministry.

Two Master Images of Ministry Leadership[13]

The Shepherd

As the human culture of the ancient Near East moved from a hunting and gathering society to a more stable nomadic and then largely agrarian

---

other, especially in program-sized and larger congregations" (personal communication, January 12, 2007).

10. The term "CEO" is of course an acronym for the "chief executive officer" of a business or nonprofit organization.

11. Other significant master images include the minister as military leader and feudal lord, both of which characterized the rise of episcopacy. I am indebted to E. Glenn Hinson, "The Church and Its Ministry," in *Formation for Christian Ministry*, ed. Anne Davis and Wade Rowatt, Jr. (Louisville: Review and Expositor, 1988), 15-28, for suggesting these categories. Hinson calls these "*models* of ministry," but I have chosen to label them "master *images*," which I believe more precisely denotes their nature and function, as well as avoids confusion with the theological models of ministry discussed later in the study. For my discussion and analysis of the meaning and value of theological models of ministry, see chapter 1 of Charles J. Scalise, *Bridging the Gap: Connecting What You Learned in Seminary with What You Find in the Congregation* (Nashville: Abingdon, 2003), 20-24.

12. For more extensive development of these models with critical comparisons that utilize both historical and contemporary case studies, see Scalise, *Bridging the Gap*. The five types of models examined in the book are correlational, contextual, narrative, performance, and regulative.

13. By highlighting these two prominent images, I am not claiming that they are the most significant and theologically justified images used in the history, but simply

one,[14] the domestication of animals played a major role. Old Testament patriarchs counted much of their wealth in "flocks and herds."[15] A web of imagery relating to sheep and the daily life of shepherds developed across the Near East.[16]

Gods and kings in the ancient Near East were commonly described as shepherds. For example, the Egyptian god Osiris is commonly portrayed holding a shepherd's crook along with a flail and sometimes is called "shepherd."[17] Isaiah 44 proclaims that the Persian king Cyrus "is my shepherd [*ro'i*],[18] and he shall carry out all my purpose" (Isa. 44:28). This purpose most importantly included the rebuilding of Jerusalem and its temple.

The common vocation of the shepherd was used by extension to describe one who cared for the multitude of God's people. Jack Vancil describes some of the Old Testament usage: "As among other ANE [ancient Near East] peoples, Israel's leaders were often regarded as shepherds, and even though God was always their principal shepherd, responsible human agents were necessary so that Israel would not be as 'sheep without a shepherd' (Num 27:16, 17); and significantly, a charismatic element

---

that they are among the most visible in the story of Western Christianity. Since the CEO model is a creation of the modern period, despite its present dominance, its historical visibility is less than that of the shepherd.

14. For an overview of the archaeological, societal, and cultural development of Israel during these early periods, see Emmanuel Anati, "The Prehistory of the Holy Land (until 3200 B.C.)," and Hanoch Reviv, "The Canaanite and Israelite Periods (3200-332 B.C.)," both in *A History of Israel and the Holy Land,* ed. Michael Avi-Jonah (New York: Continuum, 2001).

15. The Hebrew word *tson,* most commonly translated "sheep or flock," but also referring less frequently to small cattle or goats and metaphorically to a "multitude," occurs more than 260 times in the Old Testament. For examples of the various uses, see Francis Brown, S. R. Driver, and Charles A. Briggs, eds., *A Hebrew and English Lexicon of the Old Testament* (Oxford: Clarendon, 1972), 838. In Genesis alone, note the references to "flocks and herds" in 13:5; 32:7; 33:13; 45:10; 47:1; and 50:8.

16. Jack W. Vancil, "Sheep, Shepherd," in *The Anchor Bible Dictionary,* ed. David Noel Freedman, 6 vols. (New York: Doubleday, 1992), 5:1187-90.

17. For this and many additional examples and references, see Vancil's article cited in the previous note.

18. This is strikingly the same word used for YHWH in the well-known shepherd psalm (Ps. 23:1). Note the alternative pointing that seeks to soften the dramatic reference to Cyrus to "my friend, companion" *(re'i).*

is said to have rested on such leaders (Num 27:16-21; cf. Isa 11:1-9; 44:28–45:1)."[19]

Of course, the New Testament portrays Jesus as the Good Shepherd. The imagery of shepherding surrounds the life and death of Christ, from the shepherds who heard the announcement of our Savior's birth (Luke 2:8-20) to the promise in 1 Peter 5:4 that "when the chief shepherd *(archipoimenos)* appears, you will win the crown of glory that never fades away." The most well-known and fully developed use of this imagery to describe our Lord is in John 10:1-18, where it is tied with Jesus' foreshadowing of his own sacrificial death. "I am the good shepherd [*poimen*]. The good shepherd lays down his life for the sheep" (John 10:11).

It is not surprising, therefore, that the early church described its leaders as shepherds (in Latin, *pastores*). Like the faithful shepherds of Israel, early Christian leaders were responsible "to tend the flock of God that is in your charge, exercising the oversight" (1 Pet. 5:2).[20] A shepherd's solicitude for his or her flock was smoothly and symbolically transformed into the "*pastoral* care" for a congregation. Also, early Christian leaders were clearly expected to pattern their lives after the Good Shepherd who "calls his own sheep by name" and "lays down his life for the sheep" (John 10:3b, 11b).

The image of shepherd to describe ministry has some obvious limitations.[21] On the one hand, although Christians sometimes behave like naive sheep, they are persons made in the image of God who have been redeemed by Jesus Christ. They deserve the highest respect, not condescending leadership. If not carefully qualified, the notion of persons as "sheep" can lead to disempowerment of the universal priesthood of all believers.

On the other hand, although a pastor may be wise, she or he is certainly *not* all-knowing. A "shepherd" who pretends to know exactly what is best for his "sheep" is on the road to authoritarianism. If not carefully qualified, the image of shepherd can be used to justify a centralized clergy that ignores its own sinfulness, both individually and corporately. This kind of de-

19. Vancil, "Sheep, Shepherd," 5:1189. Vancil also mentions Jeremiah's description of Israel's enemies as shepherds (Jer. 6:3; 12:10; cf. 13:20) and the use of the "evil shepherd theme" in Ezek. 34 to portray "selfish, irresponsible," and oppressive leadership.

20. Several important ancient manuscripts do not have the Greek *episkopountes,* translated above as "exercising the oversight."

21. For a related discussion of this theme, see Seward Hiltner, *Ferment in the Ministry* (Nashville: Abingdon, 1969), 103-5.

velopment may help to account for the church borrowing images of military commander and feudal lord to describe the "higher *ranks*" of ministry.

North American pastoral theology in the middle of the twentieth century provided some critical reflection on the master image of the minister as shepherd.[22] Seward Hiltner sought to reorganize Protestant understanding of pastoral ministry through "the shepherding perspective."[23] This approach attempted to resolve the tension between "pastor" as a name for the minister's overall role and the specific work, among other tasks, of "pastoral care" or "shepherding."[24]

Hiltner's *The Christian Shepherd* played a key role in the modern development of the shepherding image in Protestant ministry in North America. Hiltner claimed that the "shepherding perspective" is founded on the basis of the gospel and so is "unique to Christianity."[25] He asserted that "the essential meaning and significance of shepherding . . . is seen pre-eminently in the story of the Good Samaritan."[26] He emphasized that the *healing* dimension of the pastoral task, rooted in Christ's command to heal, is the central function of the shepherding perspective on ministry. Since the Lord Jesus is "that great shepherd of the sheep" (Heb. 13:20 KJV), Hiltner proclaimed that "we are to act as shepherds, that is undershepherds, under the commission to preach and to heal."[27]

Hiltner's vision of leadership in ministry combines his shepherding

22. Although this study focuses upon Seward Hiltner's employment of the Christian shepherd image, for some more recent discussion in Anglo-American pastoral theology, see Alastair V. Campbell, "The Courageous Shepherd," in *Images of Pastoral Care: Classic Readings,* ed. Robert C. Dykstra (St. Louis: Chalice, 2005), 54-61.

23. Hiltner sought to describe formally the discipline of pastoral theology in his *Preface to Pastoral Theology* (Nashville: Abingdon, 1958).

24. In *Ferment in the Ministry* Hiltner describes nine functional images of ministry: preaching, administering, teaching, shepherding, evangelizing, celebrating, reconciling, theologizing, and disciplining.

25. Seward Hiltner, *The Christian Shepherd: Some Aspects of Pastoral Care* (Nashville: Abingdon, 1959), 14-15. Hiltner argued, "Other high religions have spiritual directors of one kind or another who deal with people as individuals or in small groups. But dealing with people in terms of shepherding, the essence of which looks toward healing in a holistic sense, is unique to Christianity and Judaism, and even in Judaism its development since biblical days has been quite different from that in Christianity" (15). Of course, Hiltner's writing during this period reflects the post–World War II religious "revival" in mainline American Protestantism (12).

26. Hiltner, *The Christian Shepherd,* 15.

27. Hiltner, *The Christian Shepherd,* 15.

perspective with "communicating the gospel" and "organizing the fellowship."[28] This threefold model of leadership shaped much of the teaching of pastoral care and practical theology[29] until the rise of contextual paradigms in the 1980s and 1990s that continue to dominate the field today.[30]

Hiltner maintained that a shepherding perspective, which carefully avoided ineffective "attack and denunciation," could move ministry leaders from cultural conformity toward theonomous (God-ruled) ministry.[31] Despite the limitations of its male-centered, individualistic focus, Hiltner's effort to use the image of "shepherd" as a focus for healing the

28. In part IV (pp. 173-215) of *Preface to Pastoral Theology,* Hiltner formally examines the perspectives of "communicating" and "organizing" as "cognates" to the discipline of pastoral theology.

29. See, for example, the dominance of the view of "minister as pastoral director" in Niebuhr, *Purpose of the Church,* 79-94. Although many of the applications of Hiltner's shepherding perspective on ministry belong exclusively to his mid-twentieth-century North American context, one insightful example has significant relevance to our contrasting images of the minister as shepherd and business executive. Hiltner's work appeared shortly after William Whyte's famous social psychological study, which popularized the term "the organization man" (William Whyte, Jr., *The Organization Man* [New York: Simon and Schuster, 1956]). Hiltner observed that American culture encouraged church leaders to become "ecclesiastical organization men" (Hiltner, *The Christian Shepherd,* 99-103). Of course, in the twenty-first century the pattern of "ecclesiastical organization women" may also be found. Hiltner argued, "If a minister is an organization man, it is because he permits the actual church to have heteronomous control over him" (101). One cannot help but notice the polarizing nature of this relationship, which is a far cry from the "mutual ministry" of pastor and congregation. The idolatry of "success" eclipsed any capacity for self-critical leadership. Idolatrous cultural conformity, rather than prophetic leadership, characterized these ministers and their congregations.

30. John Patton, *Pastoral Care in Context: An Introduction to Pastoral Care* (Louisville: Westminster John Knox, 1993). Patton proposes a "communal contextual paradigm" to understand the discipline.

31. The threefold typology of "heteronomous," "autonomous," and "theonomous" authority was articulated by Paul Tillich. For its use in Christian doctrine, see Paul Tillich, *Systematic Theology,* 3 vols. (Chicago: University of Chicago Press, 1951-63). Hiltner analyzed the psychological situation and proposed a ministry solution: "Since organization men, even in the ministry, are products of fear and insecurity, shepherding needs to involve helping them to find the needed security. Their need for security and for the avoidance of risk, genuine initiative, and the exercise of creativity, is shown in their being organization men. What they need is a base of security from which risk, initiative, and creativity can and must be exercised. . . . So only the man with the right security base can afford to transcend conformity" (*The Christian Shepherd,* 102-3).

fears of culturally entrapped ministry leadership points in a biblically redemptive direction.

The Business Executive

Christianity in England and America is well known for its creation of and reliance upon a host of "religious organizations."[32] Among evangelicals, this perspective is most apparent in the flourishing of parachurch ministries[33] of every conceivable — and sometimes inconceivable — variety.[34] H. Newton Malony candidly identifies the cultural predominance of a business understanding of religious organizations — and thus of ministry leadership — in America. "Although scholars assert that religion is one of the major institutions in every society — the other two being family and government — the fact is that religion is more like a business than a family. . . . Religious organizations survive or fail according to the same rules that govern every business on every corner. . . . I am convinced that religious leaders who conceive of their roles in purely religious terms will never achieve full effectiveness."[35]

The global cultural predominance of market capitalism creates pervasive pressure on churches and their ministers to succeed — "achieve full effectiveness" — or else face the threat of organizational extinction.[36]

32. See Mark Noll, *The Old Religion in a New World: The History of North American Christianity* (Grand Rapids: Eerdmans, 2002); Nathan Hatch, *The Democratization of American Christianity* (New Haven: Yale University Press, 1989).

33. Douglas A. Sweeney, *The American Evangelical Story: A History of the Movement* (Grand Rapids: Baker, 2005), especially 74-75.

34. For example, Fuller Seminary has recently experienced the creation of a break-dancing group for Christians.

35. H. Newton Malony, *Living with Paradox: Religious Leadership and the Genius of Double Vision* (San Francisco: Jossey-Bass, 1998), xiii-xiv. Malony goes on to argue that the religious leaders "who succeed best are those who face the paradoxes in their environment and attempt to live with the double truths they represent" (xiv). In some ways Malony's view of "double truths" seems to revive a theme from the minority medieval tradition of Latin Averroism. For more on this see Saint Thomas Aquinas, *On the Unity of the Intellect against the Averroists (De Unitate Intellectus Contra Averroistas)*, ed. James H. Robb, trans. Beatrice H. Zedler, vol. 19 of *Mediaeval Philosophical Texts in Translation* (Milwaukee: Marquette University Press, 1968).

36. For a popular critique of this theme, see Eugene Peterson, *Under the Unpredictable Plant: An Exploration in Vocational Holiness* (Grand Rapids: Eerdmans, 1992).

So, contemporary culture both creates and strongly reinforces the business executive image for ministry, which clearly identifies the senior pastor or sole pastor as the CEO.

The leadership development consultant Reggie McNeal describes the recent rise of the manager and CEO images of ministry in America:

> With the rise of organizational life in American culture came the rise of management and management science, which has more recently morphed into the field of organizational behavior. The church has followed the complexifying trend of American organizational life, and the church leader has had to become at least minimally competent in the areas of personnel management, facilities planning, budgeting and fundraising, and program administration, to name a few. In more recent years the function of CEO became part of the leadership portfolio with the rise of megachurches.[37]

McNeal incisively describes how the images of manager and CEO followed the rise of American-led international business culture and of the information industry that supports its ideology. He claims to see the re-emergence of "apostolic leadership" and advocates that it replace the manager and CEO understandings of ministry. Yet McNeal reveals his continuing dependence on the business executive images when he admits: "Business leaders have to stay in touch with the culture to survive, so their insights inform apostolic leaders' entrepreneurial bent of developing ways of taking the gospel to the marketplace."[38]

Contemporary culture both creates and strongly reinforces the business executive image for ministry, which clearly identifies the senior pastor or sole pastor as the CEO.

McNeal's use of terms like "entrepreneurial bent" and "marketplace" in discussing what is supposedly an emerging "apostolic" image for ministry reveals the continuing predominance of the image of min-

---

Peterson sadly observes, "Somehow we American pastors, without really noticing what was happening, got our vocations redefined in terms of American careerism" (20).

37. Reggie McNeal, *The Present Future: Six Tough Questions for the Church* (San Francisco: Jossey-Bass, 2003), 124.

38. McNeal, *The Present Future*, 127.

ister as business executive. The apostles of the New Testament faced the challenge of *physical* survival — not merely *organizational* "survival" — when they proclaimed the Christian message. Despite McNeal's desire to move away from "the institutional church in North America" toward a more apostolic model attuned to the generational diversity of postmodernity, he cannot escape the dominant metaphors of the entrepreneurial culture in which he lives. Even an insightful consultant cannot transcend the cultural shaping of his language and thought.

As participants in a materialist entrepreneurial culture, evangelical Christian leaders in North America who think they are called to become "apostolic leaders" need to recall our Lord's admonition to the New Testament apostles: "It is easier for a camel to go through the eye of a needle than for someone who is rich to enter the kingdom of God" (Mark 10:25; Luke 18:25).

The recent adulation of "America's New People's Pastor," Rick Warren, offers one highly visible example of the influence of the business executive image in ministry. Although Warren personally has sought to avoid being understood in the successful business executive mode, the CEO image clearly dominates the following description (complete with a page-length photo portrait) of Warren as the first of *Time* magazine's "twenty-five most influential evangelicals."

> These are heady times for Rick Warren. His book *The Purpose Driven Life* . . . has sold more than 20 million copies over the past two years and is the best-selling hardback in U.S. history. When he took the podium to pray on the final night of Billy Graham's Los Angeles crusade at the Rose Bowl in November, the 82,000 congregants cheered as if Warren had scored the winning touchdown. And on the eve of the presidential Inauguration, Warren, who pastors the 22,000-member Saddleback megachurch in Lake Forest, Calif., delivered the Invocation at the gala celebration. Later he met with 15 Senators, from both parties, who sought his advice and heard his plan to enlist Saddleback's global network of more than 40,000 churches in tackling such issues as poverty and ignorance.[39]

39. David Van Biema, "The Twenty-five Most Influential Evangelicals in America: Rick Warren, America's New People's Pastor," *Time,* February 7, 2005.

One can compare this contemporary acclamation of Warren with the ancient adulation of Ambrose of Milan (ca. 339-397), found in Augustine's "best-selling" *Confessions.* Like Warren, Ambrose was a world-famous religious leader for a newly empowered religious majority (post-Constantinian Catholics).[40] Augustine (354-430) was a skeptical former Manichean at the time of his first meeting (384) with the esteemed bishop: "unto Milan I came, to Bishop Ambrose, a man of the best fame all the world over, and thy [God's] devout servant [*pium cultorem tuum*]; whose eloquent discourse did in those days plentifully dispense [*ministrabant*] the fatness of thy wheat, the gladness of thy oil, and the sober overflowings of thy wine unto the people. To him I was led by thee, unknowing, that by him I might be brought to thee, knowing it."[41]

Like Warren, Ambrose was a world-famous religious leader for a newly empowered religious majority.

Both descriptions of these highly regarded "people's pastors" reflect not only their public popularity, but also the specific historical contexts that culturally shape Christian understandings of ministry. Even though Ambrose is preaching in a major Roman city and following the classical patterns of "eloquent discourse," he is portrayed as a pastor whose ministry can be described using the agricultural metaphors (wheat, oil, wine)[42] of the Scriptures. These images sharply contrast with the commercial and athletic metaphors used to describe Warren. The latter's predominant focus upon numbers reveals the big business of American media. Warren's success is expressed in the numbers, rather than in the "eloquent discourse" of the "devout servant" (or dutiful worshipper) of God.

40. Besides the quotation in the text, Augustine later also describes Ambrose's fame among the powerful in the following way: "As for Ambrose himself, I esteemed him a very happy man according to the world, whom personages of such authority so much honored [*quem sic tantae potestates honorarent*]." *St. Augustine's Confessions,* trans. William Watts (1631), 2 vols., Loeb Classical Library (Cambridge: Harvard University Press, 1989), 6.3, 272-73.

41. *St. Augustine's Confessions* 5.13, 254-55.

42. The Latin *cultorem,* used to mean "worshiper or supporter," has the root meaning of "one who bestows care or labor upon a thing, an elaborator, a cultivator" and commonly denotes a husbandman, tiller, or planter. C. T. Lewis and C. Short, *A New Latin Dictionary* (New York: Harper and Brothers, 1879), 488. The eucharistic symbolism of Ambrose's agricultural metaphors is also clearly visible here.

Theological Models for Comparing the Shepherd and the CEO

One helpful way to compare these master images of "the shepherd" and "the business executive" in the practice of Christian leadership is by using models that connect theology and ministry. In the remainder of this study we will analyze the impact of shepherd and CEO images upon ministry through the lenses of three theological models: correlational, contextual, and regulative. We will briefly summarize each model and then offer a comparative analysis of the model's perspective of the shepherd and CEO images.

A Correlational Model

Correlational models for integrating theology and ministry seek to connect human questions and needs, commonly described by other disciplines like philosophy and psychology, with the traditions of the Christian faith. Paul Tillich pioneered the development of this method in theology. In Tillich's approach theology "makes an analysis of the human situation out of which the existential questions arise, and it demonstrates that the symbols used in the Christian message are the answer to these questions."[43]

Tillich's method is unidirectional, as it moves from the philosophical questions of human existence to the symbols of the faith. David Tracy proposed, instead, a method of "mutually critical correlation" between interpretations of the Christian classics and the lived experience of faith communities.[44] This created a genuine two-way dialogue between theology and other disciplines.[45]

43. Tillich, *Systematic Theology,* 1:62. Tillich offers an introductory discussion of his method at 1:59-66.

44. Tracy develops this method in his *Blessed Rage for Order: The New Pluralism in Theology* (Chicago: University of Chicago Press, 1975) and *The Analogical Imagination: Christian Theology and the Culture of Pluralism* (New York: Crossroad, 1981). He applies this method to practical theology in "The Foundations of Practical Theology," in *Practical Theology: The Emerging Field in Theology, Church, and World,* ed. Don S. Browning (San Francisco: Harper and Row, 1983). For a helpful introductory overview, see Werner Jeanrond, "Correlational Theology and the Chicago School," in *Introduction to Christian Theology: Contemporary North American Perspectives,* ed. Roger A. Badham (Louisville: Westminster John Knox, 1998).

45. Don Browning used this method to develop a structure for the field of practical

A correlational model is an awkward fit with the image of the minister as shepherd. While some have attempted to correlate the practice of shepherding with ministry, they have generally generated only proverbs or aphorisms, like "Shepherds lead rather than drive!"[46] This difficulty, which highlights the distance between the ancient biblical culture and postmodernity, helps to account for the restriction of the shepherd image to historical studies of ministry[47] and the classics of pastoral theology.[48]

A mutual correlational model is a natural fit with the master image of the minister as business executive. Scripture and the traditions of the Christian faith are correlated with the disciplines of management science and organizational behavior. Among many Protestant Christians, especially evangelicals, the correlation may be understood as connecting Christian discipleship and leadership. Christian leaders who follow the CEO image are able to correlate their theology with the many contemporary resources of the social sciences to advance its understanding. As the abundance of books on Christian leadership demonstrates, the correlational model reveals differences between groups and promotes dialogue with current cultural themes and trends.

Yet a correlational model risks the subordination of aspects of the gospel that are critical of the pervasive culture of big business and the media. Both the historical traditions of the Christian ministry[49] and the pro-

---

theology. Don S. Browning, *A Fundamental Practical Theology: Descriptive and Strategic Proposals* (Minneapolis: Fortress, 1991).

46. Hinson, "Church and Its Ministry," 22. For a devotional approach in this style, see W. Phillip Keller, *A Shepherd Looks at Psalm 23* (Grand Rapids: Zondervan, 1970, 2005), and Don Baker, *The Way of the Shepherd: Courage and Commitment from the Twenty-third Psalm* (Sisters, Oreg.: Multnomah, 1987).

47. Among the many studies of the history of ministry, especially among Catholics, one helpful investigation of ministry in the early church is Kenneth Giles, *Patterns of Ministry among the First Christians* (Melbourne, Australia: Collins Dove, 1989).

48. See the collection of exhibits in William A. Clebsch and Charles R. Jaekle, *Pastoral Care in Historical Perspective* (Englewood Cliffs, N.J.: Prentice-Hall, 1964; New York: J. Aronson, 1983). A recent attempt to rehabilitate the tradition of classical pastoral theology may be found in Andrew Purves, *Pastoral Theology in the Classical Tradition* (Louisville: Westminster John Knox, 2001) and *Reconstructing Pastoral Theology: A Christological Foundation* (Louisville: Presbyterian Publishing Corp., 2004).

49. An informal survey of more than one thousand titles, including doctoral dissertations, on "Christian leadership" in the McAlister Library of Fuller Seminary re-

phetic dimension of pastoral ministry are easily subordinated, as the CEO pastor becomes an expert in organizational leadership. The numerically focused life of North American religious organizations predominates over countercultural biblical notions of self-sacrifice and community risk on behalf of the downtrodden and oppressed. Christ's call to take up one's cross (Matt. 16:24; Luke 9:23) is not frequently sounded in Christian leadership seminars.

A Contextual Model

All Christian ministry occurs in specific historical contexts. So, in a general sense, all theological reflection upon ministry is "contextual theology."[50] Yet, beginning in the latter third of the twentieth century, a wide variety of new approaches to global theological reflection that *highlight* context developed. The lived experience of the particular group being studied becomes the focus of attention. The tools of analysis by race, gender, and social class are commonly employed. Diversity is recognized and frequently celebrated. Yet prioritizing specific contexts limits the capacity for generalizability, and the "slippery slope" of relativism haunts this model (e.g., "what's true for me in my context is not necessarily true for you in your context").

Attending to the first-century shepherd's context, one cannot help but notice its attunement to the sacrificial protection and preservation of life. "The good shepherd lays down his life for the sheep. The hired hand, who is *not* the shepherd and does not own the sheep, sees the wolf coming and leaves the sheep and runs away — and the wolf snatches them and scatters them. The hired hand runs away *because* a hired hand does not *care* for the sheep" (John 10:11b-13, italics added).

The vocation of the minister as shepherd is characterized by care. It is not accidental that the term "pastoral care" has evolved to describe the ministry of parish clergy and chaplains. Perhaps the most fundamental

---

vealed only a handful of books that displayed any critical engagement at all with the long history and traditions of Christian ministry.

50. For an articulate expression of this view, see Stephen B. Bevans, *Models of Contextual Theology,* rev. ed. (Maryknoll, N.Y.: Orbis, 2002). My own view differs from Bevans in restricting the category of "contextual theology" to theologies that *privilege* context.

indictment of a minister is that he or she demonstrates a lack of care by his or her actions.[51]

A contextual analysis of the image of minister-as-shepherd, centered upon the issue of power, reveals some major limitations of this image. Although shepherds in the ancient world tended to be of lower social status, they were lords and masters in relation to their sheep. The shepherd, as owner of the sheep,[52] literally had the power of life and death over them.[53] As previously mentioned, the stereotype of the all-knowing shepherd and the flock of "innocent, dumb sheep," when applied to ministry, can easily lead to disrespect and even abuse. In addition, the overindividualistic focus upon the power of the shepherd to care for the sheep provides no warrant for *congregational* care. The dangerous "lone ranger" image of minister — with all its potential for destruction, both of pastors and their congregations — needs to be restrained by church structures of lay accountability.[54]

A contextual analysis of the minister as CEO plainly reveals attunement to the market context. The pastor needs to guide the congregation to discern the current needs and cultural expressions of the target audience for the church's ministry. If an appropriately affluent group is targeted and enlisted, the congregation will both enjoy financial stability and have funds to dispense for mission outreach to the less fortunate. Facilities upgrades and media events are pursued to insure the continued visibility and attractiveness of the congregation to the wider community from which it seeks to draw. These constantly changing recruitment and retention strategies are particularly important for developing a successful ministry with youth and young adults, where sophisticated marketing analysis reads the latest trends in youth culture. Recent strategic man-

51. Certainly many situations of clergy malpractice fall under this category. For a powerful narration and analysis, see Marie M. Fortune, *Is Nothing Sacred? The Story of a Pastor, the Women He Sexually Abused, and the Congregation He Nearly Destroyed* (Cleveland: United Church Press, 2001).

52. Cf. "the hired hand, who . . . does not own the sheep" (John 10:12).

53. Perhaps this is a major reason why it is appropriate to confess that "The Lord is my shepherd" (Ps. 23:1) but not always safe to proclaim that "Pastor X is my shepherd."

54. For example, the Catholic Church in the United States has recently learned the necessity of lay panels for priestly accountability in its sad experiences in the pedophilia scandals.

agement approaches are enlisted to evaluate the numerical success of the ministries of the church and the yield of its "investments" in ministry.

When the CEO ministry is fully institutionalized, the senior pastor's role[55] is primarily ensuring the numerical and financial health of the congregation as a conglomerate organization with a wide variety of "departments," led by a corps of staff ministers who enlist volunteer labor to make the community flourish. This accommodation to market-driven business culture means that ministry to the poor and needy, while an important "benevolent ministry" of the church, is far from the center of its mission and goals. In addition, powerful senior pastors, even when they are deeply committed Christians, are especially vulnerable to moral and ethical scandals that characterize the contemporary international business and media culture.

Powerful senior pastors, even when they are deeply committed Christians, are especially vulnerable to moral and ethical scandals that characterize the contemporary international business and media culture.

A Regulative Model

The final model for connecting theology and ministry that we will consider is a regulative one. A regulative model seeks to construct a cross-disciplinary analogy between theology and language. This model is an extension of the pioneering work of George Lindbeck on the nature of doctrine.[56]

When a student learns a new language in school, he or she is typically confronted with a group of grammatical rules describing the proper way to speak and write the language. What is the purpose of learning all those rules? In the overwhelming majority of situations, the goal of learning the rules is to develop the capacity to speak and write the language fluently and grammatically. For most people the goal of mastering the

55. Gender analysis, using a contextual model, reveals the power dynamics of the curious recent position of some conservative Protestant groups that allow women to serve as staff ministers but prohibit them from becoming ordained senior pastors.

56. George Lindbeck, *The Nature of Doctrine: Religion and Theology in a Postliberal Age* (Philadelphia: Westminster, 1984).

rules of grammar is not to become a grammarian or a comparative linguist. The goal is to become a competent reader, speaker, and writer of the new language. The test of whether one has mastered the rules of grammar is not whether one can recite the rules from memory, but whether one can speak grammatically.

Lindbeck's cultural-linguistic approach to Christian doctrine maintains that learning Christian doctrine works something like learning a new language. The purpose of Christian doctrine is to enable Christians to speak correctly about the teachings and mysteries of the faith. In other words, learning Christian doctrine is learning the *"grammar" of the faith.*[57] When Christians fail to follow the rules of doctrine — the grammar of the faith — then they run the danger of speaking "ungrammatically" or even incoherently about the faith. Obeying Christian doctrine is more like following a grammatical rule than it is like arguing for a proposition or expressing a religious emotion.[58]

As Jesus' famous parable of the lost sheep (Matt. 18:12-14; Luke 15:3-7) reminds us, a major purpose of shepherding is protecting and rescuing the sheep. Luke clearly expresses the analogy between rescuing lost sheep and rescuing lost sinners: "When he [the shepherd] has found it [the lost sheep], he lays it on his shoulders and rejoices. . . . Just so, I tell you, there will be more joy in heaven over one sinner who repents than over ninety-nine righteous persons who need no repentance" (Luke 15:5, 7).

The shepherd carrying the lost sheep on his shoulders became a well-known figure of early Christian art.[59] Drawing on ancient images, it

57. The philosopher Ludwig Wittgenstein spoke of "theology as grammar" in his *Philosophische Untersuchungen/Philosophical Investigations,* trans. G. E. M. Anscombe (Oxford: Basil Blackwell, 1967), 1:373. For my discussion of the significance of Wittgenstein's remark for theological hermeneutics, see Charles J. Scalise, *Hermeneutics as Theological Prolegomena: A Canonical Approach* (Macon, Ga.: Mercer University Press, 1994), especially 33-35. A related approach to philosophical theology that places Wittgenstein's remark in dialogue with Kierkegaard's thought is Paul L. Holmer, *The Grammar of Faith* (San Francisco: Harper and Row, 1978).

58. Lindbeck distinguishes his cultural-linguistic approach to Christian doctrine from both "cognitive-propositional" and "experiential-expressive" approaches. I have sought to extend and apply Lindbeck's cultural-linguistic approach to some issues in contemporary pastoral theology in Charles J. Scalise, "Agreeing on Where We Disagree: Lindbeck's Postliberalism and Pastoral Theology," *Journal of Pastoral Theology* 8 (1998): 43-49.

59. The Christian symbol of the Good Shepherd carrying the sheep on his shoul-

eventually came to portray the care of the Good Shepherd Jesus, and derivatively the care of Christian pastors, for the lost and straying children of God.[60]

The master image of minister-as-shepherd naturally fits the regulative model's emphasis upon learning through community practices. The practices of shepherding have largely been transmitted by oral tradition and through apprenticeship. One learns to herd sheep by following in the steps of other experienced shepherds. It is no accident that much early pastoral training followed this apprenticeship model, which is still utilized in supervised ministry experience in contemporary theological education. The natural way to learn the ways of Christian shepherding is to practice shepherding, under the guidance of experienced pastors, while living in Christian community.[61]

The emphasis of a regulative model upon learning about the Christian tradition can easily lead to a conservative bias that seeks to preserve the institutional status quo and its power arrangements from the challenges of prophetic dissenters.[62] The prophet Amos would be the first to admit that shepherding and prophesying were two distinct vocations (Amos 7:14-15).

In contrast, viewing the master image of minister as business executive from the perspective of a regulative model does not encourage tradition, but brings us into the conflict-ridden area of business and the law.

---

ders was adapted from the figure of the *criophorus* of the ancient Near East. According to Snyder, this symbol is "very early and extensively used": Graydon F. Snyder, *'Ante Pacem': Archaeological Evidence of Church Life before Constantine* (Macon, Ga.: Mercer University Press, 1985), 22-24. A striking ancient statue of the Good Shepherd figure is displayed at Caesarea Maritima.

60. Snyder, *'Ante Pacem,'* 22-24, argues that this development probably occurred after Constantine.

61. This raises questions for university-based practices of education for ministry that are disconnected from the daily life of communities of faith. For a thoughtful examination of many of these questions and a substantive alternative proposal, see Robert Banks, *Reenvisioning Theological Education: Exploring a Missional Alternative to Current Models* (Grand Rapids: Eerdmans, 1999).

62. For further critical discussion of Lindbeck's cultural-linguistic model of Christian doctrine, see Bruce D. Marshall, ed., *Theology and Dialogue: Essays in Conversation with George Lindbeck* (Notre Dame, Ind.: University of Notre Dame Press, 1990), and Timothy R. Phillips and Dennis L. Okholm, eds., *The Nature of Confession: Evangelicals and Postliberals in Conversation* (Downers Grove, Ill.: InterVarsity, 1996).

As any pastor who has ever faced a hostile zoning board can attest, the CEO image for ministry makes one wish for legal rather than theological training. The CEO minister is responsible to the "shareholders" of the church, whether congregational or denominational, to "protect the investment" in the enterprise. The theological vocation of Christian ministry can be easily lost amidst the legal maneuvering for organizational success. The spectacle of high-profile Christian leaders caught in scandals and prosecuted for crimes follows all too easily the recent indictments of high-profile CEOs.

Just as a CEO always needs to be aware of the constantly changing business environment, so a minister-as-CEO needs to be constantly attuned to cultural change. Much of the emerging church movement may perhaps be understood as reflecting this imperative.[63] Discovering new opportunities for ministry and new styles of ministry leadership parallels the quests of the emerging generation of business leadership. These parallels help to account for the success of easy-to-read books on Christian leadership, especially those that are thinly veiled, "baptized" versions of popular how-to-succeed-in-business publications. In short, a regulative model for connecting theology and ministry illumines the cultural captivity of many North American Christian leaders.

Conclusion

H. Richard Niebuhr and Daniel D. Williams tell us, "It is dangerous to think of the church's life in the narrow terms of any one function however meritorious in itself it may be."[64]

This brief study has explored two master images for Christian ministry — one ancient and one modern. We have historically investigated the development of the minister as shepherd, and have compared and contrasted it with the minister as business executive. We briefly described the correlational, contextual, and regulative models for connecting theology and ministry and then analyzed critically the strengths and weak-

63. For some empirical research and discussion of the emerging church movement, see Eddie Gibbs, *ChurchNext: Quantum Changes in How We Do Ministry* (Downers Grove, Ill.: InterVarsity, 2000) and *LeadershipNext: Changing Leaders in a Changing Culture* (Downers Grove, Ill.: InterVarsity, 2005).

64. Niebuhr and Williams, *Ministry in Historical Perspectives*, x.

ness of each image. No one of these models offered the best angle of vision to illuminate the two images. Rather, our understanding of the minister-as-shepherd and the minister-as-CEO has been deepened by examining the perspectives afforded by these and other complementary approaches.[65]

Pastors and other ministry leaders in North American culture are often confused and conflicted in their practice of ministry because they lack a core image for their ministerial identity that is supported by their faith communities. They find themselves beset with a host of conflicting expectations, reflecting a plethora of images of ministry against which they are judged. No one of these many images can fully embrace all aspects of the challenging vocation of pastoral leadership. Instead, ministers should be encouraged to construct their pastoral identity *theologically* in dialogue with Scripture, their faith communities, and personal Christian experience.[66] Rather than a pastoral ministry that is a constantly changing potpourri of images, ministers can select a core theological model to anchor their pastoral identity. Through theological analysis of their core model in specific ministry contexts, pastoral leaders can then supplement it with other models, whose strengths balance the weaknesses of the primary model. The wise eclecticism of a blended model replaces constantly shifting ad hoc images used to justify ministry.[67]

Pastors and other ministry leaders in North American culture are often confused and conflicted in their practice of ministry because they lack a core image for their ministerial identity that is supported by their faith communities.

In our analysis the historical and cultural shaping of the language that we use to understand and describe Christian ministry emerged repeatedly as a major theme. Future attempts to offer leadership to Chris-

65. Some preliminary analysis of the shepherd and CEO images of ministry using narrative and performance models has yielded similar results.

66. I have maintained elsewhere that Scripture, community, and personal Christian experience constitute the scope of authority in Protestant theology (e.g., *From Scripture to Theology: A Canonical Journey into Hermeneutics* [Downers Grove, Ill.: IVP, 1996], 20ff.).

67. For detailed discussion of this proposal, accompanied by case studies, see *Bridging the Gap*, especially 168-77.

tian communities could be significantly strengthened by careful attention to the historical contexts and theological models of Christian leadership. As the apostle Paul observed, “We have this treasure in clay jars, so that it may be made clear that this extraordinary power belongs to God and does not come from us” (2 Cor. 4:7).

3 The Reality of Your Context: Fundamental Elements and Multicultural Leadership

William A. Dyrness

Editor's Introduction Defining reality will be of limited use to us in the pastorate if we restrict ourselves to working within the reality of our limited cultural context. However, attempting to define reality outside of one's familiar cultural context can be fraught with danger. In this essay William Dyrness, who teaches theology at Fuller Theological Seminary, explores the notion of defining reality in a multicultural context. In particular, he explores the way the cultural context impacts relationality, agency, and embodiment and asserts that communities in any context are sustained by a rootedness in the trinitarian life of God.

Cultural Factors

The relationship between leadership and cultural factors is becoming increasingly important in discussions of leadership. Defining culture is certainly a critical piece of a leader's definition of reality. While missionaries in the Philippines, we were reminded many times of the way culture limited or expanded our ability to lead. An experience of a colleague has remained in my memory as a classic encounter between cultures that resulted in the failure of leadership.

One of our senior missionaries early in his career had been assigned to plant churches on one of the islands south of Manila. After holding Bible studies in homes and carrying out evangelistic meetings in various settings, he was beginning to gather a few converts around him. One day the mayor of the major town on the island came to him and said: "We have been watching you and listening to what you have said, and we have decided that we would like our town to become Christian." After a few moments of confusion the missionary managed to respond: "Well, thank you, but you do not understand. Villages don't become Christians, people do. Each person must decide for himself or herself to become a Christian." Now it was the mayor's turn to be confused. For in his culture individuals did not make decisions about anything of importance; leaders — after proper consultation — did that. In the end he went away, puzzled and probably disappointed.

Why did the missionary refuse his generous offer? Later the missionary recognized his mistake. He realized that the process of decision making had important cultural implications that he had not understood. He had learned in Bible school that people decide to become Christians individually; in rural areas of the Philippines decisions are invariably corporate affairs. The missionary, to his credit, learned from his mistake, but by then it was too late for this island region. They continued to be "resistant" to the gospel, or so it was believed.

Cultural factors are critical because they are the most intimate and personal factors that determine the leadership situation. Culture as we use it here is the continuing human response to God's project of creation and renewal. It is the communal, active, embodied engagement with God's purposes as these are furthered or distorted by human rebellion. Both in pain and in glimpses of greatness, human practices necessarily embody the human response to God's presence and the call of the Holy Spirit in particular social and historical settings.[1] These responses take shape in human institutions, in language, customs, and the arts, and they form our various corporate and individual identities.

Today, in most places in the world, leadership is practiced within a multicultural situation, since no culture exists in isolation, or in a form uninfluenced by surrounding cultures.

Leadership is exercised and shaped within values of particular cultures. Today, in most places in the world, this means leadership is practiced within a multicultural situation, since no culture exists in isolation,

1. I am using a definition of culture that I have developed more fully in *The Earth Is God's: A Theology of American Culture* (Maryknoll, N.Y.: Orbis, 1996), chapter 3, "Culture."

or in a form uninfluenced by surrounding cultures. The missionary in our story had to deal not only with the cultural values of the people he lived among, but also with his own cultural assumptions — which were often invisible to him. The leader must surely take account of particular cultural realities on the ground — the caste system in India (or the term now preferred, "communities of India"), tribes in Africa, tribal minorities in China, and so on. Note first that these groupings exist within, and sometimes at odds with, various national entities. These cultural groupings moreover exist within particular power arrangements, which limit or even block the free expression of people's values. But leaders must become aware of the values and prejudices that shape their own decisions.

In addition, these factors often take shape in terms of particular topical challenges, such as expectations regarding women in Muslim cultures, the influence of popular Western culture on urban youth in Africa, and so on. Again, in both of these cases influences on local cultures are profound and inescapable. They also reflect the intercultural and global character of many of the challenges leaders face today. That same missionary returning to his island today would find an entirely new set of cultural challenges.

Cultural values determine perceptions of leadership — in the first instance, they determine what it is *possible* for a leader to do. The missionary never dreamed it was possible for a powerful leader to actually make decisions about religious priorities for people under him. How a leader is supposed to act in traditional African culture is different from how a leader is to act among educated persons in Europe. These values also determine how conflict, or difference, is managed in a particular setting. Issues of immigrant rights in Southern California pose particular challenges to leaders in that setting — both within and outside the church — as do attitudes toward, say, Indian merchants in East Africa.

What underlies all the issues related to culture is the given of human **relationality.** Human persons exist and develop within webs of relationship. The missionary assumed that relationships are constructed; the Filipino village leader experienced relationships as given in the order of society. For a Westerner, relationships are achieved; for many outside the West they are ascribed. In either case identity is formed by the cultural group to which we belong, just as it is challenged by the presence of different groups and values. In some fundamental sense leadership is about using the values and norms of culture to manage difference in a way that is constructive. Managing difference in turn reflects an underlying principle that is found in the directionality of God's nature — that God works in history to realize particular purposes. God in the historical expression of the trinitarian reality is in Christ reconciling the world, and by the Holy Spirit seeking the shalom that will one day be visible to all. Meanwhile, the human management of difference, when it is healthy, will always echo this purposive thrust in God's being.

For a Westerner, relationships are achieved; for many outside the West they are ascribed.

Fundamentally, however, the management of difference is the discovery and celebration of relationship and interrelationship. It goes without saying that leaders do not create relationship. Even when introducing someone to a stranger, they are seeking to recognize a relationship that is preexisting, because of the work and presence of God. But we argue that this recognition of the inescapable character of relationality is not ad hoc, but grounded on the trinitarian reality of God whose presence underlies the created order and is reflected in patterns of leadership that promote human flourishing in any and all cultures. But this relationality is not static, as the older functional sociologists had it, but directional. It seeks redress, wholeness, and reconciliation, which leads us to the next set of factors in the exercise of leadership.

If leadership is fundamentally about managing relationship, it is equally about managing process and change.

Culture and Process

If leadership is fundamentally about managing relationship, it is equally about managing process and change. Liberation theology may not be thought to have contributed much to our understanding of leadership, but it clearly helped us understand the nature of social change — or perhaps I should say, the necessity of social change. When Gustavo Gutiérrez began speaking and writing about theology in the early 1970s, he made two observations about Latin America in particular.[2] On the one hand, he realized that received understandings of social science explained relationships in functional terms. Culture was understood as a closed system that reflected deep and long-lasting structures. Family structures, economic patterns, even religious practices were all determined by long-standing structures and values embedded in culture — a fact well illustrated by our Filipino leader.

The problem with this static view of society was evident from the second observation that Gutiérrez made about Latin America. In most countries of Latin America the largest percentage of the population was poor, and more importantly, since World War II their situation was growing worse. In other words, in spite of the belief that society as a functional reality was unchanging, social change was in fact taking place before their eyes, and it involved a deterioration of the situation of most of the population of Latin America. As he noted, "Social conflict — including one of its most acute forms: the struggle between social classes — is a painful historical fact."[3] Gutiérrez's development of liberation theology was his attempt to respond to this as a Christian theologian and more importantly as a pastor living and ministering in Rimac, a slum of Lima, Peru.

Gutiérrez's response was to insist that the gospel had to include some dimension of liberation. Since relationships are never static but always involve power differentials that affect those relationships and that determine the processes of culture, the Christian cannot remain indifferent to these changes. A critical part of the Christian view of relationships is that they are broken and disordered. This means that relationships, given the differences in power, necessarily create processes that can injure as well as bless.

Relationships, given the differences in power, necessarily create processes that can injure as well as bless.

When one reflects on leadership, the implications of this attention to process are obvious: leadership must be in part an intervention into process; it inevitably implies **agency**. From one point of view our missionary was trying to emphasize the necessity of personal agency in religion —

2. See his classic work *A Theology of Liberation,* trans and ed. Caridad Inda and John Eagleson (Maryknoll, N.Y.: Orbis, 1973).

3. Gutiérrez, *A Theology of Liberation,* 157.

the mayor was trying to locate agency in traditional terms. In terms of the New Leadership movement, leadership represents the ability to formulate and communicate a vision in such a way as to "build trust and create commitment."[4] That is, to mobilize the gifts and interests of the community in the direction of a desired goal. Two notions appear in the New Leadership quote above that demand comment: communication and trust. Note first that leaders direct and manage a process of communication. Within a changing situation, which is constant and ongoing, the leader begins by defining reality. But now, more specifically, we are arguing that reality itself is in process, it is changing and moving in some direction or another, and the leader has to define and confront the reality of this process. This act of definition is not simple, nor is it done once and for all. It is itself a mobilization of insight and perspective that the community offers, but shaped in the form of a vision of what is happening and what should happen, that all who hear it will accept. From one point of view the encounter of my missionary friend with traditional structures is a classic case of the way cultural encounters should result in mutual change and influence. Both leaders were correct in the cultural terms in which they understood leadership; neither was capable of understanding how these patterns might affect each other.

But note further that for leaders to manage processes, they must work within an atmosphere of trust. Agency cannot be activated apart from a trust that the view of reality being presented is honest and appropriate, and that the leader will respond in helpful and constructive ways, even if specific interventions are not immediately appreciated.

Billy Graham displayed a good example of the exercise of agency in a leader early in his career, when he was faced with the challenge of whether to hold integrated evangelistic rallies. During the early 1950s he held integrated rallies in the north and segregated rallies in the south — a practice that was common and widely understood. But as he traveled he broadened his contacts with the black community and grew increasingly uneasy with this practice. In 1952, during a campaign in Jackson, Mississippi, he decided to take dramatic action. At the beginning of the first meeting he personally removed the ropes that divided the sections. As a mystified

4. Pierluigi Piovanelli, "Jesus' Charismatic Authority: On the Historical Applicability of a Sociological Model," *Journal of the American Academy of Religion* 73, no. 2 (2005): 419, 420.

usher tried to put them back up, Graham himself stopped him. "The ground is level at the foot of the cross," he told his Mississippi audience. He never held another segregated meeting.[5] Here was a dramatic intervention that illustrated the agency that is necessary to direct processes. Many factors went into the situation he faced, but what matters is that this was not a static reality, but a process involving the dynamic interaction of many factors, including communication and the mobilization of trust. Leadership demands an agency that understands the reality and complexity of these processes and itself becomes an appropriate force within these events.

Embodying Culture

Clearly relationship and agency are interrelated. Relationships are the context in which agency is exercised, and agency is the process by which direction is introduced into relationships. Both reflect the mutuality that existed in cultural relationships and the flows and counterflows those relationships create and call for. If one represents the notion of the field in which leadership is exercised, the latter introduces the notion of the force that the field exercises and the response that is demanded.

But something critical is missing from the description of the context if these two are the only realities. What is missing, I argue, is the objective or material factors with which leadership must deal. In every situation there is always a range of material, human, and natural resources available to communities and organizations. The normative category that this dimension implies is what I call **embodiment**. That is, relationships and processes never exist in the abstract but always in particular forms and shapes that partake of specific resources, either of materials or of time. The response to this reality that Scriptures call for is stewardship, which is the appropriate care and use of the material and human assets available.

Unblinking focus on raising funds leads us frequently to save money and spend people.

5. Harold Myra and Marshall Shelley, "Jesus and Justice," *Christianity Today,* August 2005, 58. This article is taken from the book by these authors, *The Leadership Secrets of Billy Graham* (Grand Rapids: Zondervan, 2005).

Every context of leadership provides certain resources that leaders and their associates may appropriate. This may also be referred to as the economic context, in the broad sense of the word. For economics properly is not simply the organizing of financial resources, but it is the managing of all kinds of scarce resources. In fact, I would argue that focusing simply on financial constraints is to misconstrue the larger challenge of stewarding a broader range of social and natural resources that is available. Leaders that focus unblinkingly on the raising of funds, for example, implicitly deny that relationships and processes are equally important to leadership and the healthy functioning community, and that use of resources takes place in and affects these relationships and processes. As a colleague said, such an imbalance leads us frequently to save money and spend people, rather than to steward all resources in such a way that their values are enhanced.

Again the context of embodiment is a created order in which people, goods, and time exist in dynamic interrelationship with persons and cultures. Here the best example is the ministry of Jesus himself. Even when performing miracles, he always began with the resources available: at Cana he asked the steward to fill the jars with water; at the feeding of the multitude he began with what was provided, the small boy's lunch. Whether the harvest will be thirtyfold or a hundredfold, we must begin by sowing the seed that we have. But note that the call to the rich young ruler to sell everything began not only with the recognition of what was there, but also with *how this mattered* to the man — that is, Jesus recognized the dynamics of the resources in their human setting. Jesus understood that even the processes of the kingdom began with what was there and that you cannot deal with people apart from the goods and resources they bring with them and the way these define people's existence.

A moment's reflection indicates how impossible it is to define resources in the abstract. The wealth of a given culture has to do with a great deal more than simply its economic or natural resources, though these are clearly important. It has to do with practices and values that Pierre Bourdieu calls symbolic capital. In fact, he argues that considering economic resources more narrowly is a kind of ethnocentrism, ignoring as it does the subtleties of the forms of gift economy.[6] Western visitors to

6. See Bourdieu, *The Logic of Practice*, trans. Richard Nice (Palo Alto: Stanford University Press, 1990 [1980]). He notes that economics is based on pure mistrust; gift economy on pure trust (115)!

Africa are frequently struck by the generosity and hospitality of people of meager means. The point is, the resources exist in a dynamic system of values and relationships in which they find their meaning. Leadership, in part, is the exercise of stewardship and discernment in recognizing and exploiting resources. But it also calls for leaders to exercise this discernment in the highly charged environment of human need and ambition. Every culture offers a unique blend of resources and values, and, to be sure, special needs and opportunities for growth and development.

Conclusion

Might it not be possible to speak of sustainable human communities in a similar way? Could it be that sustainable communities are those that learn consciously to experience their rootedness in the trinitarian life of God, and by their worship practices to enhance that relationship? This would involve not only learning dependence on God, but also the grace to reflect God's own loving relationships and mutuality in their ongoing communal life together. Understanding leadership in terms of this divine context would surely change the way we develop and select our leaders, and it would also prepare us to learn much about the various cultural contexts in which we are called to work.

Let us return to our narrative from the Philippines. Suppose the missionary had understood and accepted the fact of traditional relationships and the leadership patterns that resulted. Suppose, that is, he understood and appropriated the symbolic capital that these patterns embodied. If he had accepted these realities, instead of resisting them, he might have responded by saying something like this: "This is wonderful news. Now this is what we should do for these people to better understand what this important decision means. Let us have them meet regularly in their neighborhoods. We can instruct them in the faith, they will learn to worship and pray together, and we will learn much from them." In doing something like this he might have better realized the relational character of the social reality; he might have encouraged a process that gave each neighborhood, each family, and eventually each person a sense of agency; and finally, by the grace of God, he might have seen the visible evidence of the body of Christ take root in that place.

4 Defining Institutional Realities: The Myth of the Right Form

Sherwood Lingenfelter

Editor's Introduction Defining reality is a heady idea for new pastors. It carries with it notions of creative expression, if not power and influence. However, for many pastors it is a sobering moment when they realize they must face the reality of the organizational structure of the church to which they have been called. This can lead to a kind of crisis if they wonder whether the reality of their church structure is the "right" one. In this essay Sherwood Lingenfelter, the provost at Fuller Theological Seminary, challenges the notion that there is a "right" form of church structure. Lingenfelter asserts rather that pastors can faithfully apply wisdom from wise teachers in a variety of institutional structures.

What place does structure play in appropriate leadership for a congregation? Among students that I have encountered, most of those in preparation, and many already engaged in ministry, are seeking the "right structure" that will enable them to achieve their ministry mission and goals. Most established denominations, and even independent and "emergent" churches, have formal structures of governance that limit a leader's options, and yet local elders and congregations adapt those structures to local talent and vested interest groups. It is almost a given that a new pastor will reflect on the organizational structure of a local ministry and propose changes toward "greater effectiveness." The argument of this chapter is that leaders and congregations often misplace confidence in organizational structure, believing it a critical feature of ministry success. Defining reality for many congregations may mean helping people to abandon their reliance upon structure and process and to concentrate on cultivating vibrant faith, vision, and covenant relationships. This chapter will first critique the notion of a biblical norm for church structure, and then address the essentials for extraordinary leadership, employing any organizational form.

Does Scripture teach a normative or "right form" for the church? In the contemporary debate about leadership for the church in the twenty-first century, many scholars and significant church leaders have proposed different answers to this question. Rick Warren suggests that the "purpose-driven church" must have a simple structure in which the pastor leads, the staff does maintenance, and the people do ministry.[1] Saddleback has no committees, no board, no voting; governance is managed by a senior staff team that answers to the pastor, while ministry is led by sixty-nine or more lay leaders who are supported and led by staff. C. Peter Wagner sees Warren's governance approach as too corporate, arguing for a "second apostolic age" in which spiritual warfare is the mission of the church and "apostolic generals" have vertical authority from Christ to lead people and networks in a spiritual warfare against the evil forces of our time.[2]

Defining reality for many congregations may mean helping people to abandon their reliance upon structure and process and to concentrate on cultivating vibrant faith, vision, and covenant relationships.

Howard A. Snyder, in contrast, rejects all "hierarchical forms" and judges megachurches, microchurches, and business models as biblically inadequate dead ends.[3] He argues that the church is "the covenant community of God's reign" and that "healthy covenant communities teach and practice plural leadership." Borrowing from ecology, he defines covenant groups as organic rather than organized entities and he rejects ordination and the distinctions of clergy/laity.[4] Snyder's views are not new; Robert L. Saucy argued that plural elder leadership is the "normative"

1. Rick Warren, *The Purpose Driven Church: Growth without Compromising Your Message and Mission* (Grand Rapids: Zondervan, 1995), 375-80.

2. C. Peter Wagner, *Changing Church* (Ventura, Calif.: Regal, 2004), 115-18.

3. Howard A. Snyder with Daniel V. Runyon, *Decoding the Church: Mapping the DNA of Christ's Body* (Grand Rapids: Baker, 2002), 62ff.

4. Snyder, *Decoding the Church*, 52-56.

structure for church leadership and taught this throughout his forty-year career at Talbot Theological Seminary.[5]

There are, thus, substantive disagreements about how best to mobilize and organize congregations for mission. Some (such as Wagner and Saucy) have argued that their view is biblically supported and normative, and when a person or group of persons exercise leadership through that form, then under the power of the Holy Spirit the mission of the church will naturally flow. I reject the notion of a "right form" and will briefly outline why.

A Historical Perspective

Craig Van Gelder provides a succinct review of the significant changes in the doctrines and forms of the church from the first century to the present.[6] He notes that between A.D. 50 and A.D. 300 Christians experienced much persecution, which forced believers to move from place to place, meeting in a house, in a synagogue, or in larger settings as the circumstances permitted. As a consequence, they employed varying forms of assembly and leadership, adopting place and structure as needed to meet together.

From my reading of the Scriptures, Acts 2–4 suggests egalitarian (all equal) house and temple groups in the city of Jerusalem right after Pentecost. Then very quickly, as the church spread through persecution, Christians adapted to the cities into which the church grew. Acts 15 suggests that James was recognized as head of the church in Jerusalem and that leaders met in council to hear disputed matters. That council suggests some similarity to the Jewish Sanhedrin, with the apostles having a key role. After consultation, James articulated a decision and sent out delegates to communicate that decision broadly to new churches, illustrating some hierarchy and organiza-

In the early church people assembled for worship and prayer in varying forms and contexts.

5. Robert L. Saucy, *The Church in God's Program* (Chicago: Moody, 1972).

6. Craig Van Gelder, *The Essence of the Church: A Community Created by the Spirit* (Grand Rapids: Baker, 2000), 47-72.

tion at work. Later in Acts (17) Paul met with a group of new believers in the house of Lydia; later still (Acts 24) Luke reports the gathering of a group of elders at Ephesus who came to bid farewell to Paul — a gathering that many declare different from the council in Acts 15 in Jerusalem. So, in the early church people assembled for worship and prayer in varying forms and contexts.

Van Gelder reports that Constantine's solution in the third century (making church an official part of the empire) resulted in the formalization of structures — each major city having a central church and a bishop.[7] Local and global councils of bishops framed the legitimacy and unity of the church as part of the empire. In 325 the Council of Nicea drafted the Nicene Creed — the first doctrinal statement of the church — which was formally adopted at Constantinople in 381. The Nicene Creed defined the essential characteristics of the church — one holy catholic apostolic church — which has served as the foundational ecclesiology to the present.

The formula "one holy catholic apostolic church" had specific meanings in the context of the fourth century, but these meanings have varied through time. Figure 1 provides a framework for understanding this change. The figure illustrates four quadrants through which I will reflect upon the historical progression of forms of the church. "Grid" in the figure refers to the strength of hierarchy and "group" refers to the strength of community.[8]

In the period of the Holy Roman Empire, the hierarchy of apostolic authority, formulated in the Council of Nicea, provided the integrating structure of the one holy catholic apostolic church. The bishops traced the line of authority from Peter, especially in Rome, and after the schism of East and West the authority of the pope ruled a hierarchy of bishops to govern the Western church[9] (see fig. 1).

Until Rome separated from the Eastern bishops over papal authority, the councils understood the church as united — "*one* holy church" — in obedience to the command of Jesus in John 17. Because God is holy, the church was also holy, sanctified by Jesus as his bride (Eph. 5), as revealed

7. Van Gelder, *Essence of the Church,* 50.

8. Mary Douglas, "Cultural Bias," in *In the Active Voice* (London: Routledge and Kegan Paul, 1982), 183-254; Sherwood G. Lingenfelter, *Transforming Culture: A Challenge for Christian Mission* (Grand Rapids: Baker, 1998).

9. Hans Küng, *Christianity: Essence, History, Future* (New York: Continuum International Publishing Group, 1994; reprint 2004), 382-85.

in the Holy Scriptures to us. The sacraments of the church expressed this holiness, and the church restricted the administration of the sacraments to those ordained by the bishops and the reception of those sacraments to those baptized into the church. In the eighth century the council of bishops added the phrase "the communion of the saints" to the doctrine of "one holy catholic apostolic church." This phrase emphasized the importance of community and congregation.

Figure 1. Theological and Structure Variation in the Church

Apostolic Authority Hierarchy of bishops One = unity of church Holy God, Scriptures Sacraments Communion of saints	+ G R I D	**Reformation Confession** *Sola Scriptura* "True or false" church Pure doctrine & polity Ordained ministers Sacraments
– GROUP		GROUP +
Essential NT church Worshiping community Social contract, members Denomination leaders & agencies **Voluntary Organizations**	G R I D –	Radical Reformation Redeemed community Priesthood of believers Piety leads to mission **Free Church Movement**

While the medieval church had much diversity (most specifically expressed in the monastic orders), the dominant structure was the hierarchy that emanated from Rome. As the hierarchy became increasingly powerful and corrupt, would-be reformers made numerous attempts to reform or break away from Rome. With the advent of the Reformation in Europe, the Reformers rejected the pope and the hierarchy. They replaced apostolic authority with *sola Scriptura* and they de-emphasized or even left out the phrase "apostolic church."[10]

10. Van Gelder, *Essence of the Church*, 55.

The reformed commitment to *sola Scriptura* created a significant theological dilemma — how to adhere to the scriptural command for unity. Since the Reformers had rejected and split away from the Catholic Church, how could the church be united? Van Gelder suggests that this dilemma was resolved through the notion of the invisible church as opposed to the visible church; that is, the body of Christ is represented anywhere by the believers of Christ.[11] For the Reformers the true church, the invisible church, was indeed one and united. But there were false congregations that were not part of the true church. The church of Rome was a false church, even anti-Christ, thus explaining how Reformers could and must break away to reestablish the true church of the Lord Jesus Christ. From that time the notion of "true church" and "false church" has played a key role in ecclesiology.

Another shift in emphasis focused on the "holy." The Reformers rejected the "holiness" associated with hierarchy and sacraments and replaced it with an emphasis on the purity of doctrine and polity. Working from Scripture, one studied to discern correct doctrine and define pure polity for the life of the believer and the church.[12] The leaders remained separate from the laity because they defined pure doctrine and polity for the church. Further, ordained leaders alone could perform the sacraments. Hierarchy, then, persisted in Reformed churches through the ordained administering the sacraments and teaching right theology and church practice (fig. 1). While the Reformers gave greater emphasis to the communion of the saints, even to the point of empowering laity for ministry, those not ordained were excluded from these privileged roles and from the "sacred" ministry of the church.

The Reformation succeeded in large part because of support from wealthy rulers in northern Europe. Very quickly, as these rulers broke away from the Holy Roman Empire, the Reformed churches became state churches, ruled by a new hierarchy. The Lutheran church became the state church of Germany, Denmark, Norway, and Sweden; the Reformed church became the state church of Switzerland and parts of Germany; and the Church of England extended to Scotland, Wales, and part of Ireland.

However, for many Reformers these state churches were another compromise of the "true church." The Free Church Movement (fig. 1) rejected the state and its religious hierarchy and gave much more privilege

11. Van Gelder, *Essence of the Church,* 56.
12. Van Gelder, *Essence of the Church,* 57-58.

to the communion of the saints. Known as the Radical Reformation, the Free Church Movement emphasized the redeemed community. Focusing on personal conversion and believer baptism, the redeemed community lived transformed lives in response to the call of God. Asserting the priesthood of all believers, many empowered mature believers to offer communion, baptize new believers, teach Scripture, and participate in any of the other sacramental activities of the worship of the church.[13]

The Pietistic Movement in Germany and Europe fueled this Radical Reformation. Conversion and commitment of one's life to personal piety and ministry became the markers of the redeemed community. Individuals who had a deep relationship with God inevitably expressed their faith through active engagement in worship and mission. The Moravian movement in Germany launched one of the earliest post-Reformation mission movements. A variety of different Anabaptist and Free Church movements emerged across Europe, sharing this focus on redeemed community, the priesthood of believers, personal piety, and missional action based upon the grace and mercy of God.

The Enlightenment and the birth of modernism in Europe and America had a profound impact on the church. Van Gelder notes how John Locke's idea of "social contract" framed a new ethical and moral basis for social relations that led to social communities based on voluntary association and contract.[14] The idea of voluntary membership and social contract became the rallying cry for American republican democracy. The town hall meeting served as the place for public discourse, and the rule of majority the principle for public life. These principles of individual choice and shared governance were soon transferred to congregations and the life of the church. Church became a community of social contract in which individuals decided to join, members agreed to accept them, and the community formed structures and rules of governance that guided their collective congregational life.

Many new denominations emerged in this American cultural milieu that promoted the formation of voluntary associations for community life.[15] One of the classical illustrations is the Stone-Campbell Movement (Churches of Christ), which at its founding sought to replicate the New

13. Van Gelder, *Essence of the Church,* 59-60.
14. Van Gelder, *Essence of the Church,* 67.
15. Van Gelder, *Essence of the Church,* 68-69.

Testament church.[16] The voluntary congregations in this movement defined themselves as autonomous, local congregations made up of people who embraced the restoration theology taught by Campbell and Stone and who practiced Christianity as they believed it was taught in the book of Acts. All other expressions of church (Catholic and Reformation) were false churches, apostate, whereas these congregations sought to restore the true church of Jesus Christ. They focused on voluntary worshiping communities that had a deep relationship with Christ and practiced a faith that returned to its New Testament roots.

Literally hundreds of denominations have emerged from this Enlightenment foundation of voluntary social contract. They share in common the idea that participation is voluntary, that a return to New Testament teaching is essential, and that other groups have failed to achieve this ideal. Emphasizing worshiping community, revival, and evangelism, they create new forms of organization that facilitate the expansion of their "true" church.

Today we use "denomination" broadly to speak of the many forms of church in the United States. The "mainline denominations," such as Lutheran, Reformed, and Anglican churches, trace their history to the Reformation. The early Anabaptists of the Radical Reformation split away from the Lutheran and Reformed churches. Others, such as the Presbyterian, Baptist, Methodist, and Brethren movements, emerged from the first revivals of their early Reformation traditions. Charles Wesley, brother of John, was deeply opposed to leaving the Anglican Church. John Wesley was not quite as worried about it, but he was deeply committed to the poor — organizing the poor, motivating them, and engaging them in ministry. Wesley didn't intend to start a new denomination, but out of this, Methodism emerged as a voluntary organization.[17]

Through this brief review of the history of the church we see that the church has adopted the full range of social forms in its history, reflecting all four of the theoretically possible forms of social integration and emphasis.[18] All these expressions exist today, with even more diverse social and theological expressions of faith and practice. So which is the "right form"?

16. Leroy Garrett, *The Stone-Campbell Movement: The Story of the American Restoration Movement* (Joplin, Mo.: College Press, 1992).

17. Mark Noll, *The Rise of Evangelicalism: The Age of Edwards, Whitefield, and the Wesleys* (Downers Grove, Ill.: InterVarsity, 2003).

18. Michael Thompson, Richard Ellis, and Aaron Wildavsky, *Cultural Theory* (Boulder, Colo.: Westview Press, 1990).

The "Right Form" for Missional Churches?

As we look at the Protestant literature on church growth, church renewal, and missional church, we find scholars proposing one of these various forms as biblical and as best for restoring the church to its mission. We have already seen how Snyder challenges the orthodox formulation of "one holy apostolic catholic church."[19] The missional church is not one but diverse, and while the church is universal (catholic), it is also local, and its local-ness is very different from its catholic-ness. Finally, the church is not apostolic, but instead a covenant community of priests in which every person in the church serves as part of the priesthood on mission. Snyder embraces the egalitarian covenant fellowships (fig. 2) of the Radical Reformation.

Figure 2. Structural Variation in American Protestant Churches

Authoritarian Leadership	+	**Corporate Leadership**
Megachurches		*Denominational Churches*
Big-pastor vision	G	Corporate vision
Big-pastor $$ power	R	Board controls $$, vision
Big-pastor agenda, control	I	Specialist agenda, control
Purse-string accountability	D	Corporate accountability
– GROUP		GROUP +
Independent Churches	G	*Covenant Fellowships*
Pastors' visions	R	Congregational visions
$$ flow to visions	I	Consensus on $$
Team agendas, controls	D	Local agenda, control
Accountable to God		Group accountability
Influence Leadership	–	**Rotating Leadership**

19. Snyder, *Decoding the Church.*

Other Protestants offer different formulations. For example, Saddleback and Willow Creek embrace variations of what Wagner calls "apostolic authority" leadership. Warren, in his purpose-driven church and purpose-driven leadership, focuses on a new form of apostolic leadership, claiming spiritual authority from Christ to oversee lay members engaged in ministries and reaching their communities for Christ.[20] While they reject papal succession, they adopt a similar top-down structure (fig. 2) in which purpose-driven leaders guide purpose-driven churches.

Alan J. Roxburgh, focusing on the postmodern generation, defines the North American church in terms of two tribes: the "liminals" of *denominational* churches (fig. 2) whose purpose and future are in question, and the "emergents" who have rejected all traditional forms and are creating *independent* house churches or new church plants (fig. 2) that nurture teams that lead diverse ministries.[21] Roxburgh notes the weaknesses of these divided and often chaotic local expressions of church and proposes to call these diverse expressions into a missional community. Led by an abbot/abbess, a "missional order" of a voluntary association of local congregations, house churches, and new church plants would share a common vision and diverse gifts, and agree together on rules of prayer, silence, study, and witness that guide their mission to a local community.[22]

Extraordinary Leadership for Any Form!

What is the right form? Perhaps the criteria for good leadership are not formal or structural. Rather, leadership is how one lives within a structure and how one engages people and structures for common goals. Leadership is about engaging people and structure in ways that transform yet sustain relationships and purpose.

This particular take on corporate leadership may just as readily be applied to church leadership. We have already seen that denominations are built upon similar principles of social contract and voluntary association. Leadership in many denominations is corporate — role-focused,

20. Warren, *The Purpose Driven Church.*

21. Alan J. Roxburgh, *The Sky Is Falling!?! Leaders Lost in Transition* (Eagle, Idaho: ACI Publishing, 2005), 19ff.

22. Roxburgh, *The Sky Is Falling?!?* 182-83.

power-directed, and success-driven. Biblical leadership does not require that we convert corporations and corporate structures into egalitarian fellowships of equals. Rather, wise leadership focuses on relationships and values — grounded in the principles of Christian faith — that transform corporate leadership and community.

Leadership is how one lives within a structure and how one engages people and structures for common goals.

One of these principles is covenant relationship. Corporate leaders may see their people as participants in covenant community — not egalitarian, as Snyder proposes, but rather committing to one another as people, agreeing to support one another.

Max De Pree used to come into the corporate office in the morning and have a conversation with one of the janitors. Every day he greeted this man and chatted briefly about his family and work. One day he came in and the janitor was missing. Thinking he was sick, he didn't say anything. But the next day the janitor was still missing. After several days De Pree contacted one of his vice presidents and asked about the missing janitor. The vice president said he wasn't very productive, so he dismissed him. De Pree fired the vice president and rehired the janitor. Why? Because of covenant relationship.

When people have committed to us, we are committed to them. And whereas they might not always be the most productive people, God hasn't gifted all people to have the same productivity. So for De Pree, his duty as leader was to love the people that God had brought to the corporation, and even if they weren't the most gifted or the most productive, to keep this mutual covenant of relationship.

Yet, a covenant relationship is not one that lacks accountability or focuses on productivity. The janitor or team member must be accountable, and a good supervisor will let that person know when he or she falls short and offer guidance on how to improve. But an employee or a team member knows the leaders' commitment to him or her as a person.

Max De Pree made it very clear that Herman Miller was not a democracy but a corporation. Leaders make decisions for the good of the corporation and its people. But one doesn't live by the power-focused culture of profit-centered corporate cultures. Rather, a leader changes the rules of participation to reflect inclusiveness, commitment, and communication.

Biblical "Form" or Biblical "Leadership"?

The point is, wise leadership does not abolish corporate hierarchy, but transforms it with the art of leadership. If corporate or church leaders play their roles as social contract — role-focused, power-driven, and power-directed — that behavior distorts and destroys. If, on the other hand, one leads out of covenant relationship, inclusiveness, commitment, and communication, the corporate or congregational relationships are transformed and become something useful in the plan of God for humanity.

How does this principle apply to the question of "the right form" of church leadership? In the historical and contemporary review above, I have illustrated that every expression of the church embraces at least one "prototype social game." In the theory first articulated by Mary Douglas, all social life is framed on one or more of these four essential prototypes.[23] Each prototype is based upon fundamental social choices about grid and group that have inherent "social game values." For example, to choose individualism (weak grid and weak group) is to give priority to the individual over others, resulting in a competitive and continuously changing social environment. Some values inherent to each social prototype counter the kingdom values of Christ. The social game values of a corporation are not kingdom values. A good leader should seek to bring kingdom values into his or her corporation.

Church organizations of every type are no different from corporate or other social organizations — by embracing one set of social variables over another, they embrace social values that often counter kingdom values. All social types are vulnerable, limiting God and mission to "our spirit-revealed" social game. Mission becomes "our vision," finance is for "our strategy," controls are to assure "our outcomes," and accountability is to assure "our standard of quality." The illusion that seduces all leaders and followers is that we have the "right form" for God's work, and we trust the form and system rather than God. Leaders become power seekers rather than servants in the work of the Master, i.e., the mission of God.

H. Stanley Wood has conducted research on the most effective church planters in seven mainline denominations, seeking to ascertain

23. Lingenfelter, *Transforming Culture.*

the leadership characteristics that result in new, growing churches.[24] Wood's data confirms the point made here, that biblical and visionary leadership results in growing churches. Wood notes that the three most important characteristics to start a new church are a vibrant faith in God, vision, and catalytic innovation. The catalytic innovator is a self-starter, an innovator, a risk-taker, and tenacious and charismatic.[25] Once the church is established, the leader has many of the same characteristics De Pree describes for a corporate leader — a passion for people, for sharing faith, and for empowering others. The effective leaders have healthy relationships with those in the congregation and inspire people through preaching and worship. While Wood does not speak of covenant relationship, the characteristics he describes are very similar to those De Pree uses to define covenant relationship.

In conclusion, the critical factor in healthy, growing churches is Christ-centered leadership. When leaders are passionate about their faith in God and follow Jesus in their love and care for their people, when they are motivated by the mission of God and bring this vision to their people, when they commit to covenant relationships with those who follow and give away power rather than seek it, the people follow as the leader follows Christ and the church becomes a powerful force of the transforming mission of God in their world.

24. H. Stanley Wood, ed., *Extraordinary Leaders in Extraordinary Times: Unadorned Clay Pot Messengers* (Grand Rapids: Eerdmans, 2006).

25. Wood, *Extraordinary Leaders,* 34-37.

5 The Pulpit as Primary Setting for Defining Reality

Earl F. Palmer

Editor's Introduction One of the assumptions of this volume is that leadership in the corporate realm can be exercised in a variety of settings. This includes the pastorate. However, preaching pastors have, in the pulpit, a forum for exercising leadership that is without parallel in other spheres of society. Sadly, many pastors fail to comprehend the unique privilege and responsibility of the pulpit and far too often try to get by with shoddy preaching. In this essay Earl Palmer, pastor emeritus at University Presbyterian Church in Seattle, reminds pastors of the unique privilege of this forum for exercising pastoral leadership. Palmer strikes a healthy balance between the privilege of a weekly uninterrupted conversation and the responsibility of being a faithful interpreter of Scripture and being a teachable pastor.

Imagine this: there are people who, more or less regularly, are willing to listen to a Christian pastor without the chance to talk back or ask questions. That event each Sunday lasts from twenty to thirty minutes, usually within an hour of public worship in a Christian church. These minutes are called the sermon. The people in the congregation are present by personal choice, and the gift they offer to a pastor is from twenty to thirty minutes of their attention as they listen to the sermon of the day. This gift itself is a compelling human mandate to a preaching pastor to steward those minutes so that the people's gift is honored and their time is not wasted. But preaching the gospel is a mandate from the Lord of the congregation, and therefore preaching a sermon is a divine imperative too. That reason for preaching compels a pastor to share the gospel of Jesus Christ and the biblical sources for the gospel in the texts of the Old Testament and New Testament so that both preacher and people may encounter the implications of that good news as an encouragement for our daily living as Christian people.

These two obligations, one from the people and one from the Lord of the people, converge in the sermon. Because of each a pastor needs to be well prepared through regular study of the biblical texts so that the sermon teaches and gives witness to the truth faithfully. The pastor also needs to study the people and their world so that the sermon wisely relates the biblical truth of the law and the gospel into and alongside the listeners' place and time so that the message is accurate, timely, and persuasive. The sermon needs the inner depth of biblical and theological wholeness that is sourced in the biblical texts. The sermon also needs homiletic skillfulness so that its content is communicative and understandable.

Two obligations, one from the people and one from the Lord of the people, converge in the sermon.

The preacher must never take these thirty minutes lightly, because if they are wasted, the penalty is the loss of the listener's attention. This loss, in a Protestant congregation, where the preaching of God's word is a highly valued event, is a very grave loss.

What then should happen in the sermon if these two mandates, one from the people and one from the Lord, are to be fulfilled?

A few weeks ago I was interviewed by a university student who was writing a paper on career options and choices. The student asked me what I found rewarding in my career as a Protestant minister. I shared with the student that the two most rewarding ingredients in my post as the senior pastor at University Presbyterian Church (UPC) were, first, the chance to watch people of all ages grow in grace as they grow in age, to see the gospel of Jesus Christ make sense to people, men and women, young and old, and then to watch them mature in discipleship. This is the great joy of Christian ministry.

The second joy of the ministry is to preach each Sunday to the people. Think of it! As a pastor I have the honor of deciding what our people are going to think about week by week. Our worship tradition at UPC is to preach expositionally through Scripture. For example, this past winter we, as UPC pastors, preached through the book of Matthew. This meant that my colleagues, as members of the pastoral staff, joined with me as we journeyed with our people through Matthew's Gospel. The pastors knew their assigned texts weeks in advance, and our people were provided a printed study guide to aid in their personal or small-group study of Matthew. We titled the series of sermons "Meeting Jesus Christ in the Book That Matthew Wrote." My privilege and responsibility as senior pastor was to decide that we as a congregation would journey through Matthew's Gospel from Advent to Easter. This meant that the themes in his book were on all of our minds during those weeks. Following Easter of 2006, we, as a congregation, considered for ten weeks a series of sermons we titled "The Great Commandment and the Great Commission: Ministries of Hope That Change the World." This journey took us through various texts that focused on these two grand mandates of Jesus Christ. When the sermons' goals are put into place, it becomes possible to design special classes and small-group study opportunities that parallel and are related to the Sunday worship preaching.

I believe that the sermon each Sunday should play a vital role in the congregation of stirring up the imagination of the people and their desire for further personal study and inquiry into subject matter that is historical, biblical, theological, and most important, is an encouragement for growth in discipleship. The sermon may even become a catalyst for artists and poets, writers and musicians in the church encouraging young and old to express their own imaginative and creative responses to themes that were made real to them in the Sunday preaching. I have observed that these powerful possibilities are the most evident when preaching is committed to enabling the texts of Holy Scripture to make their own themes clear and understandable. For this reason I believe thoughtful, expositional preaching is the most relevant and needed in today's church. I mean by that the exposition that enables the biblical texts to speak into the contemporary setting of the present-tense listener with wisdom and warmth and practical application.

A serious danger to preaching today is what I call the thematic captivity of the sermon.

But there is a crisis in contemporary preaching and worship leadership. I believe that a serious danger to preaching today is what I call the thematic captivity of the sermon. By this I mean the sermon that is primarily thematically focused rather than expositionally focused. Its theme may be faithfully rooted in Christian convictions or perhaps the pastor's experience, or the pastor's prophetic advocacy. But the sermon and often the worship that surrounds it derive their message source from these general truths and personal journey sources, and though the intent may be soundly orthodox, nevertheless the listener hears truths of Christian faith told from personal authority. The preacher may even underline these themes by story narratives of his or her own life experiences, but what is missing is that essential connection between a Christian truth such as love or hope or faith and the biblical source where it is rooted so that the hearers of the sermons are enabled to see this profound connection. The great moment in a sermon is that electric instant when a text from Scripture is unfolding and a person in the pew sees the connection before the preacher says it. The person sees it because it is there in the text, not because a pastor assured the person the pastor was sure it was true.

I remember one Sunday when I and my daughter, Anne, a university student at the time, listened to a sermon together on the radio. The sermon was about hope. The preacher had read Romans 8:18-25 as his text, but he made no reference to that text throughout his sermon. He told inspiring stories from his life where he found hope in Christ and then made an evangelistic appeal at the close of the message to encourage his listeners to trust in Jesus Christ, who gives us hope. Following the service my daughter asked me what I thought of the sermon. I said I appreciated the warmth of the pastor and that I was personally moved to tears by one of the illustrations. She was not influenced by what I said. She told me, "Dad, I didn't like the sermon because the pastor said, 'You should have hope because I have hope,' and Dad, that is not a substantial enough source for the gospel." She was right. What a moment it might have been if Saint Paul's great text in Romans 8:18-25 had been allowed to speak and we could have experienced our own breakthrough moment of realization; our hope would then have been rooted in the text of the gospel and not only in the warmhearted experience of the pastor. For our experiences of grace we are grateful and they encourage us, but our experiences are not the message of the gospel. The gospel has its own integrity and truth *extra nos* (outside ourselves). It is precisely because of this objective reality that the gospel is relevant and joyous good news *intra nos* (inside ourselves).

A pastor who is careful in teaching the text should also bring these same skills into the pastoral/leadership mandate that calls upon the preacher/pastor to be a realistic observer of the people. What I mean is that the skill of exegeting a biblical text is not that different from the skill needed in exegeting news from the *New York Times*, the movies people are watching, and the common daily life experiences of the people in our congregations. A pastor needs to be a student of language to understand texts but also to understand people. C. S. Lewis said it best: "Tell me what the hard words mean and you have done more for me than a thousand commentaries." The biblical realism that enables a preacher to faithfully interpret the texts of the Bible will also enable a pastor to wisely interpret the cultures of people and also to observe the limitations on interpretation so that a sermon does not drift into either careless, mild generalizations or carelessly bold statements that are without adequate check and balance.

The preacher in a Christian church needs the healthy restraint of measured fairness, especially when he or she speaks from the pulpit, since hearers ordinarily cannot answer or interrupt the sermon. Therefore that unequal relationship on a Sunday morning requires that the pastor exercise self-restraint. This care for fairness and respect will protect the pastor from carelessness and misuse of the high privilege of the pulpit. When that self-restraint is practiced, the result is the earned respect of the thinking parishioner even if there are convictional differences of opinion between a congregant and the minister. Fairness and openness to correction when that is necessary are lifestyle markers that describe an effective prophetic preacher. The irony of the prophetic role in preaching is that the more dogmatically assertive a pastor becomes in moral and social advocacy, the less persuasive the pastor is with the people who occupy the not-all-black, not-all-white middle place on the issue. Advocacy that comes from a preacher who has a track record for carefulness and accuracy is listened to with less defensiveness. When a pastor has earned the respect of the people as a thoughtful teacher, then that pastor is able to teach the people through the territory of the disturbing crosswinds of confusion and falsehood. The leadership and prophetic goal for each of us pastors is to teach our people through error and to teach our way into the healthy territory of truth and grace. Because pastors in the biblical tradition of Christian leadership have understood our ministry as teachers of the word, teaching should be our primary strategy for change and renewal. It may appear to be a slower strategy for change, but it has the advantage of wearing well over the long journey, and it is a fact that the result is more lasting for those who are convinced by truth they discover themselves.

This approach is slower, but it is also less endangered by panic and overprotection. It is a more creative way to face up to crisis, and it is more in keeping with the tradition of the New Testament epistles. "We teach our way through error" is respectful of the complexity present in most social and theological issues. It invites a long-term journey for our people in facing up to social realities and it at heart trusts in the gospel of Christ to keep us centered. This is important because one of the most destructive aspects of social advocacy is that the specialized advocacy itself may develop its own life and inner dynamic so that fellow Christians are judged and even condemned by how they relate to a particular issue at hand. The advocacy then in a subtle way has replaced the centeredness of christological wholeness. Jesus is moved away from the center to the margins, and the particular missional or prophetic concern is now the real center.

The specialized advocacy itself may develop its own life and inner dynamic so that fellow Christians are judged and even condemned by how they relate to a particular issue at hand.

We who are preachers/teachers/pastors are, ourselves, people under the gospel and believers who belong to Jesus Christ. When Jesus Christ is the true center and basis for our life and mission, then both we and our missional concerns benefit. We become more like inviters into a grand banquet who are privileged to stand at the doorway, not as judges, but as pointers. We stand on the same ground as our people. It is a level ground, and what they need most we need as well, "to grow in grace as we grow in age."

TASK 2 Servanthood

6 The Primacy of Servanthood

Siang-Yang Tan

Editor's Introduction Many people, pastors included, read books on leadership to learn the latest techniques for becoming effective leaders. If these books happen to assert servanthood as a useful strategy toward becoming a great leader, they are willing to give it a try. In this essay Siang-Yang Tan, who teaches for the School of Psychology at Fuller Theological Seminary, challenges this understanding of servanthood. If our goal is to become great leaders, then we have already missed the point, Tan asserts. Tan recommends that we aspire to do things for a great God rather than to do great things for God.

The literature on leadership, including Christian leadership, is voluminous, reflecting a widespread and sustained interest in the topic. There are also many conferences and seminars on leadership each year that pastors, church leaders, and others enthusiastically attend. Unfortunately, there has been a tendency to universally embrace secular models of leadership and management and apply them too quickly and indiscriminately to the church as well as parachurch organizations. While leadership and leadership development are important and have their rightful place in Christian ministry, such a heavy emphasis in recent years on leadership in Christian contexts may be somewhat misplaced. From a biblical perspective, servanthood or following Jesus all the way in loving obedience is more foundational and central in Christian life and ministry.

This chapter focuses on servanthood as the foundational calling of God for all Christians as devoted disciples of Jesus Christ. God has called

From a biblical perspective, servanthood or following Jesus all the way in loving obedience is more foundational and central in Christian life and ministry than an emphasis on leadership per se.

us *first* to servanthood, not leadership per se. Servanthood 101 should also be the foundational course of any leadership training program or curriculum for those who may be called by God to serve in leadership. Much of the material in this chapter has been given more comprehensive and in-depth treatment in a recent book on biblical servanthood.[1]

Servanthood

My emphasis on servanthood is deliberate. It is not an emphasis on servant leadership. Servanthood is first and foremost a way of life, not so much a way to lead!

Rick Warren, in his best-selling book *The Purpose Driven Life,* pointed out: "Thousands of books have been written on leadership, but few on servanthood. Everyone wants to lead; no one wants to be a servant. We would rather be generals than privates. Even Christians want to be *'servant-leaders,'* not just plain servants. But to be like Jesus is to be a servant. That's what he called himself. . . . It is possible to serve in church for a lifetime without ever being a servant. You must have a servant's heart."[2] True servants with a servant's heart can be described as follows: they make themselves available to serve; they pay attention to needs; they do their best with what they have; they do each task with equal dedication; they are faithful to their ministry; and they maintain a low pro-file.[3] They also have the following attitudes, according to Warren: they think more about others than about themselves; they think like stewards, not owners; they think about their work, not what others are doing; they base their identity in Christ; and they think of ministry as an opportunity, not an obligation.[4]

1. Siang-Yang Tan, *Full Service: Moving from Self-Serve Christianity to Total Servanthood* (Grand Rapids: Baker, 2006). See especially chapter 5, "Servanthood versus Servant Leadership," 47-63.

2. Rick Warren, *The Purpose Driven Life* (Grand Rapids: Zondervan, 2002), 257-58.

3. Warren, *The Purpose Driven Life,* 258-64.

4. Warren, *The Purpose Driven Life,* 265-70.

A few years earlier, in a similar view, Steve Hayner, then president of Intervarsity Christian Fellowship USA, emphasized the need for true servanthood rather than leadership per se:

> There is a growing amount of modern literature on servant leadership. But I'm not sure I agree with leadership as the fundamental concept and servanthood as the modifier. Jesus gives an unmodified call to us to be servants — serving God and serving one another. Along the way, God may also call us into specific roles of leadership. But there are no indications that obtaining those roles should be a believer's ultimate ambition. . . . Our ambition is not leadership, but servanthood. Our task is not to grow leaders, but to make disciples who will follow Jesus. Our goal is not to get out there and get things done, but to listen and obey. Our call is not to exercise power but to be faithful to our Lord and the way of the servant.
>
> How God chooses to use his servants is his concern. We may be called to lead or to follow, to exert authority or to submit, to turn our God-given gifts in one direction or another. But that is God's business. Our identity, our meaning in life, our sense of significance, and our self-worth are not to be based on the roles we fill, the power we wield, or the numbers we lead. We play to an audience of one, who loves us, affirms us, and uses us . . . we should long to hear from our God the words, "Well done, you good and faithful servant!"[5]

"Our identity, our meaning in life, our sense of significance, and our self-worth are not to be based on the roles we fill, the power we wield, or the numbers we lead."

In a recent review and Christian evaluation of current leadership approaches, Robert Banks and Bernice Ledbetter provided the following insightful comments about servanthood and servant leadership:

> Though [Robert] Greenleaf [in *Servant Leadership*] insists that a leader is a servant first and only in the wake of that service is a leader, many

5. Steve Hayner, "Playing to an Audience of One," *World Vision Today,* Summer 1998, 5-6.

> people in authority place the main emphasis on the second word (leader) rather than on the first (servant). . . . Ultimately they operate in ways that are not so much different from those of traditional leaders. Such people have co-opted the language of servant leadership for their own agendas and purposes. Sad to say, this has often been the case in the church and in many religious organizations. Overall, the word servanthood is in danger of being viewed through the distorting lens of its contemporary misuse by those in authority. It is also in danger of being viewed too little in terms of its full Christian meaning. The trouble with the phrase "servant leadership," therefore, is that though it moves away from inadequate views of leading others, it still gets the order of the words wrong. Leadership is the key term and servant is the qualifier. What we need today are not, as is so often suggested, more *servant leaders,* but properly understood, more *leading servants.*[6]

"Servant leadership" therefore can have different meanings and hence be confusing. If servanthood is used only to exercise leadership as the primary focus in so-called servant leadership, then this is an unbiblical concept. However, if "servant leadership" is used to refer to leadership that is grounded or founded on servanthood first, and hence to leaders with a servant's heart or attitude, then it can be a more biblically consistent concept. It therefore correctly and biblically refers to leaders who are servants first, or servants who are serving as leaders because of a calling and gifting specifically from God. It should be emphasized again that not all servants are called to be leaders. All leaders, however, from a biblical perspective, are already called to be servants first, and then leaders.

Servanthood is a way of life, not so much a way of leading.

Servanthood is therefore a more primary concept and calling from a biblical perspective. Servanthood is a way of life, not so much a way of leading. Servanthood, reflecting devoted discipleship in following Jesus all the way, with a genuine Spirit-inspired and Spirit-empowered servant attitude, is expressed in true service and not in self-righteous service.

6. Robert Banks and Bernice M. Ledbetter, *Reviewing Leadership: A Christian Evaluation of Current Approaches* (Grand Rapids: Baker Academic, 2004), 110-11.

Richard Foster has noted that true service that comes from a servant's heart (as contrasted with self-righteous service that is more ego-centered) has the following nine characteristics: (1) it comes from a relationship with the divine Other deep within (i.e., deep friendship with Jesus); (2) it finds it impossible to distinguish the small from the large service; (3) it rests contented in hiddenness; (4) it is free of the need to calculate results; (5) it is indiscriminate in its ministry (i.e., it serves one and all equally); (6) it ministers simply and faithfully because there is a need (i.e., regardless of feelings); (7) it is a lifestyle (i.e., servanthood for life in all of life); (8) it can withhold the service as freely as perform it; (9) it builds community.[7]

The key focus in biblical servanthood is on simply doing things for a great God, and not so much on doing great things for God.

Such servanthood, when seasoned with redemptive suffering and humility, enables us to enter more deeply into God's rest and grace. It also revolutionizes our lives and ministries in the church, in the home, and in the marketplace or workplace and school, producing fruit that will last for eternity as a result of the Holy Spirit's deep work.

While we have all been called to be servants of Jesus Christ (1 Cor. 4:1), and to follow him in the ministry of the towel (John 13:14-17), he has also called us to be his friends (John 15:15-17). The Lord Jesus has called us to servanthood that flows out of deep, loving, intimate friendship or communion with him. It is *not* servanthood out of obligation, duty, guilt, fear, or selfish motives for attention and praise, which is actually *servitude.* Servanthood is not doormat servitude or slavery to other people's whims and fancies or unreasonable demands. True servants of Jesus Christ can say no when led by him to say so, without feeling guilty. Servanthood is about serving our best friend, Jesus Christ. In so doing we experience our deepest joy and fulfillment, as we live in him and for eternity.

The key focus in such biblical servanthood is on simply doing things for a great God, and not so much on doing great things for God. When we focus on doing great things instead of on the great God, we may end up

7. Richard Foster, *Celebration of Discipline,* rev. ed. (San Francisco: HarperSanFrancisco, 1988), 128-30.

trying to be great ourselves and pamper our own egos. When we focus instead on the great God, we can rest contented in whatever he calls us to do — even if it is to do *nothing* except to waste time for God and be with him in a season of deep solitude and silence with him in prayer and in his Word, or to do *small* things with deep love for others, such as bringing some food over to a neighbor who is sick. He can also call us to do big or "great" things, but that is up to him. It is God's call, not ours. We simply obey him in loving servanthood, doing things for a great God and not necessarily doing great things for God, unless he calls us to do such big or great things. This is an essential lesson in biblical brokenness and humility that all Christians need to learn: servants as well as leaders. We should also remember that big is not equivalent to great, and greatness should not be our major focus anyway. Our main preoccupation should be the great God.

Max De Pree, an exemplary model of biblical servanthood and leadership, has authored several bestsellers on leadership.[8] In *Leadership Is an Art* he wrote: "The first responsibility of a leader is to define reality. The last is to say thank you. In between the two, the leader must become a servant and a debtor. That sums up the progress of an artful leader."[9] In another book, *Leadership Jazz,* he stated: "The *servanthood of leadership* needs to be felt, understood, believed, and practiced if we're to be faithful. The best description of this kind of leadership is found in the book of Luke: 'The greatest among you should be like the youngest, and the one who rules, like the one who serves.' The finest instruction in how to practice it can be found in *Servant Leadership* by Robert Greenleaf, a lovely grace note to the melody in Luke. . . . Above all, leadership is a position of servanthood."[10]

Leadership

While some serious dangers are associated with leadership, especially leadership that is secular in nature and based on the ego asserting itself

8. Max De Pree, *Leadership Is an Art* (New York: Doubleday, 1989); *Leadership Jazz* (New York: Currency Doubleday, 1992); *Leading without Power: Finding Hope in Serving Community* (San Francisco: Jossey-Bass, 1997, 2003).

9. De Pree, *Leadership Is an Art,* 11.

10. De Pree, *Leadership Jazz,* 10-11, 220.

and its strengths without regard to God and his eternal purposes, leadership per se is not wrong or unbiblical. However, leadership is not primary from a biblical perspective: servanthood, which is a huge part of discipleship, is more central and primary.

Biblical leadership is a calling and gift (Rom. 12:8) for *some* of us who are called to be servants first. If we are also called and gifted to be leaders, we need to serve as leaders, empowered by the Holy Spirit to "lead with diligence" (Rom. 12:8). Bill Hybels is one of the strongest advocates for such "courageous leadership," asserting that *"the local church is the hope of the world and its future rests primarily in the hands of its leaders."*[11] He goes on to issue the following challenge: "People supernaturally gifted to lead must yield themselves fully to God. They must cast powerful, biblical, God-honoring visions. They must build effective, loving, clearly focused teams. They must fire up Christ's followers to give their absolute best for God. And they must insist with pit-bull determination that *the gospel be preached, the lost be found, the believers be equipped, the poor be served, the lonely be enfolded into community, and God gets the credit for it all.*"[12] Hybels also describes ten major leadership styles, emphasizing the need for leaders who develop their strong leadership styles to also grow in their weak leadership styles: visionary, directional, strategic, managing, motivational, shepherding, team-building, entrepreneurial, reengineering, and bridge-building.[13]

Hybels stresses that the single most important aspect of leadership involves the art of self-leadership that helps leaders to overcome the "dark side" of leadership that can become toxic and destructive. Crucial self-leadership questions that need to be asked regularly by leaders include: Is my calling sure? Is my vision clear? Is my passion hot? Am I developing my gifts? Is my character submitted to Christ? Is my pride subdued? Am I overcoming fear? Are interior issues undermining my leadership? Is my pace sustainable? Is my love for God and people increasing?[14]

A number of other books on leadership from a more Christian or biblical perspective have been published since Hybels wrote *Courageous*

11. Bill Hybels, *Courageous Leadership* (Grand Rapids: Zondervan, 2002), 27.
12. Hybels, *Courageous Leadership*, 27-28.
13. Hybels, *Courageous Leadership*, 139-59.
14. Hybels, *Courageous Leadership*, 181-97.

Leadership in 2002, and since Robert Banks and Bernice Ledbetter provided their helpful Christian evaluation of current leadership approaches and models in *Reviewing Leadership* in 2004.[15]

Several years ago John Maxwell, a prolific writer in the area of leadership and Christian leadership, distilled the vast leadership literature into his well-known twenty-one irrefutable laws of leadership and subsequently described the twenty-one indispensable qualities of a leader, including servanthood.[16] Whether these twenty-one laws of leadership are really irrefutable or whether the twenty-one qualities of a leader he describes are really indispensable is open to question and debate. But he does provide much food for thought.

A number of more general books on leadership have also recently been published. For example, John Wooden and Steve Jamison wrote *Wooden on Leadership* (2005), focusing on the fifteen fundamental leadership qualities or building blocks of Wooden's well-known Pyramid of Success (i.e., industriousness, friendship, loyalty, cooperation, enthusiasm, self-control, alertness, initiative, intentness, condition, skill, team spirit, poise, confidence, and competitive greatness).[17] Jack Welch, former CEO of General Electric, or GE, with Suzy Welch in their book *Winning* (2005), described what secular leaders do: "leaders relentlessly upgrade their team, using every encounter as an opportunity to evaluate, coach, and build self-confidence; leaders make sure people not only see the vision, they live and breathe it; leaders get into everyone's skin, exuding positive energy and optimism; leaders establish trust with candor, transparency, and credit; leaders have the courage to make unpopular decisions and gut calls; leaders probe and push with a curiosity that borders on skepticism, making sure that questions are answered with ac-

15. For example, see Harold Myra and Marshall Shelley, *The Leadership Secrets of Billy Graham* (Grand Rapids: Zondervan, 2005); Eddie Gibbs, *LeadershipNext: Changing Leaders in a Changing Culture* (Downers Grove, Ill.: InterVarsity, 2005); Henry Klopp, *The Leadership Playbook* (Grand Rapids: Baker, 2004); Tom Mullins, *The Leadership Game* (Nashville: Nelson Business, 2005); Wayne Hastings and Ron Potter, *Trust Me* (Colorado Springs: WaterBrook, 2004).

16. John C. Maxwell, *The Twenty-one Irrefutable Laws of Leadership* (Nashville: Nelson, 1998), and *The Twenty-one Indispensable Qualities of a Leader* (Nashville: Nelson, 1999).

17. John Wooden and Steve Jamison, *Wooden on Leadership* (New York: McGraw-Hill, 2005), 2.

tion; leaders inspire risk taking and learning by setting the example; leaders celebrate."[18]

Eric Yaverbaum recently authored *Leadership Secrets of the World's Most Successful CEOs* (2006), based on interviews with 100 top CEOs. Here is his list of the top fifteen leadership strategies of the world's most successful CEOs:

1. Have a clear vision, a specific direction, and a goal for your organization.
2. Focus on the two or three things most important to your vision and goals. Don't spread your attention too thin.
3. Communicate your vision, strategy, goals, and mission to everyone involved.
4. Listen to what others tell you. Be willing to accept and act upon criticism and suggestions.
5. Surround yourself with the right people, a strong team.
6. Treat your employees exceedingly well. Help them become successful in their careers and their lives.
7. Apply the Golden Rule: Do unto others as you would have others do unto you.
8. Be in a business you love and are passionate about.
9. Constantly innovate to gain and sustain competitive advantage and serve your customers better.
10. Plan everything. Leave nothing to chance.
11. Be a leader and actually *lead.* Take responsibility. Make tough decisions.
12. Lead by example.
13. Listen to the people who are closest to the customers and marketplace. They will give you your best advice and input.
14. Set performance goals and establish metrics by which you can measure your performance and results.
15. Be service-oriented.[19]

Marcus Buckingham, in *The One Thing You Need to Know: About Great Managing, Great Leading, and Sustained Individual Success*

18. Jack Welch with Suzy Welch, *Winning* (New York: HarperBusiness, 2005), 63.

19. Eric Yaverbaum, *Leadership Secrets of the World's Most Successful CEOs* (New York: Barnes and Noble, 2006), 257.

(2005), recently emphasized that great leaders possess two essential talents needed to rally people to a better future: optimism and ego. He concludes that the one thing crucially needed in great leadership is *clarity:*

> Effective leaders don't have to be passionate . . . charming . . . brilliant . . . possess the common touch . . . be great speakers. What they must be is clear. Above all else, they must never forget the truth that of all human universals — our need for security, for community, for clarity, for authority, and for respect — our need for clarity, when met, is the most likely to engender in us confidence, persistence, resilience, and creativity.
>
> Show us clearly whom we should seek to serve, show us where our core strength lies, show us which score we should focus on and which actions must be taken today, and we will reward you by working our hearts out to make our better future come true.[20]

Such focused clarity in great leadership will require insight, discipline, and courage.[21]

Jim Collins, the well-known author of *Good to Great,*[22] was interviewed in the Spring 2006 issue of *Leadership.* He had just published a thirty-five-page monograph, *Good to Great and the Social Sectors,* and he spoke on the implications for churches. When asked how he would define "greatness" in a church, Collins replied:

> Greatness does not equal bigness. Big is not great and great is not big. In fact, the bigger you become the harder it may be to remain great.
>
> For my purposes, an organization must have three things to qualify as great:
>
> 1. Superior performance relative to its mission in the world.
> 2. A distinctive impact on its community.

20. Marcus Buckingham, *The One Thing You Need to Know: About Great Managing, Great Leading, and Sustained Individual Success* (New York: Free Press, 2005), 197.

21. Buckingham, *The One Thing,* 285.

22. James C. Collins, *Good to Great: Why Some Companies Make the Leap — and Others Don't* (New York: HarperBusiness, 2001).

3. Endurance. Making an impact over a long enough time, so that it's not dependent on the personality of one leader.[23]

Collins also emphasized that goals need not be quantifiable but they need to be describable and hence still clear and able to be assessed. When asked what role leadership plays in great churches, Collins said:

> One of the things from *Good to Great* that really resonated with church leaders was the Level 5 Leadership finding, that leaders who took companies from good to great are characterized by personal humility and by a fierce dedication to a cause that is larger than themselves.
>
> I was delighted how the Level 5 concept took hold, and yet the deeper I got into it, the more I realized that Level 5 Leadership looks different in a non-business setting. A church leader often has a very complicated governance structure. There can be multiple sources of power, constituencies in the community, and constituencies in the congregation. With all of that, you're going to run into trouble if you try to lead a church as a czar. Church leaders have to be adept in a more communal process, what we came to call "legislative" rather than an "executive" process.[24]

I have deliberately made reference to some recent key leadership publications and cited several of them so that the range of views on leadership can be sampled. The dangers of some of these views are also obvious, especially those that emphasize the ego and an obsession with greatness, success, self-effort, and self-sufficiency. I would like to conclude this chapter with some further biblical reflections and perspectives on leadership, as well as on servanthood, that emphasize faithfulness (1 Cor. 4:2) and fruitfulness in Christ (John 15:5) rather than success or personal greatness.

Max De Pree, in the insightful article "Leadership and Moral Purpose," pointed out the need for moral purpose as a sign of God's presence in leadership. Such leadership is characterized by authenticity, inclusiveness, truth, vulnerability, access, and personal restraint, all of which are

23. "The Good to Great Pastor: An Interview with Jim Collins," *Leadership*, Spring 2006, 48-49.

24. "Good to Great Pastor," 50.

further marks of true servanthood.[25] It is clear from his writings that he advocates a leadership approach that is founded on servanthood first, with a solid, biblical moral purpose.

For leadership to be more truly Christian and biblical, a distinct difference between it and most of the secular models of leadership is crucial. Jeffrey Greenman has provided the following powerful and challenging conclusions about the contours of Christian leadership from a biblical perspective:

> One of the most powerful biblical texts about the shape of Christian leadership is Mark 10:32-45 — Jesus teaches that the cross determines the nature of authentic leadership. Throughout the New Testament, leadership is cruciform — literally, "cross-shaped." Leadership is defined as suffering servanthood precisely because Jesus' cross defines the meaning of service. . . . The cross-shaped pattern of Christian leadership is every bit as radical today as it was 2,000 years ago. Still today our culture gravitates toward patterns of leadership oriented by dominance, control and power. . . . When Christians become "squeezed into the world's mold" of leadership, or even deliberately adopt the world's leadership pattern, we abandon the way of the Cross and thereby compromise our distinctiveness. . . .
>
> Everything that is true of a disciple is also true of a Christian leader. The necessity of discipleship is intensified dramatically for those giving leadership to God's work in the world. Leaders are first and foremost disciples, people whose identity is found in the crucified Jesus. . . .
>
> Christian leaders are people who live the Cross — humbling themselves; voluntarily divesting themselves of their rights and privileges; trusting not in their own wisdom; insisting not on their own way; doing nothing out of selfish ambition; seeking not their own advantage but the benefit of others; in humility, considering others better than themselves; giving up their lives for the sake of the lost, the vulnerable, and the neglected. . . . If this is the normative pattern of leadership, it means that the crucial question for each leader is: how far are you willing to go in your discipleship?[26]

25. Max De Pree, "Leadership and Moral Purpose," *Hospital Health Services Administration* 39, no. 1 (Spring 1994): 133-38.

26. Jeffrey P. Greenman, "The Shape of Christian Leadership" (revised version of in-

Christian leadership must therefore be fully grounded in discipleship that is cross-shaped or largely servanthood-shaped. Eugene Peterson has similarly written: "Christian leadership is built on a foundation of followership — following Jesus. For those of us who are in positions of leadership — our following skills take priority over our leadership skills. Leadership that is not well-grounded in followership — following Jesus — is dangerous to both the church and the world. In our Scriptures, following is far more frequently addressed than leading. The person we follow is the primary influence on the leader we become. Christians follow Jesus."[27]

"Leadership that is not well-grounded in followership — following Jesus — is dangerous to both the church and the world."

Bill Hybels gave a powerful closing message on the topic "When the Laws of Leadership and Discipleship Collide" at the Leadership Summit 2004. There are times when the so-called laws of leadership in general will conflict or collide with biblical teachings on discipleship. Hybels was clear that at such times the laws of discipleship should always take precedence and priority over the so-called laws of leadership. Laws of leadership are therefore not always irrefutable, and qualities of leaders are not always indispensable. Hybels shared that the more he leads, the more dependent he has learned to be on the Holy Spirit, who is the leader's best friend. Hybels therefore concluded that the Holy Spirit is crucial in leadership and discipleship. I fully agree here with Hybels. I believe that the Holy Spirit is truly "indispensable and irrefutable" in leadership and discipleship, and in life itself.

Conclusion

I would like to conclude this chapter on servanthood and leadership by sharing the following words I wrote on servanthood in the church:

---

augural address on February 10, 2004, as the R. J. Bernards Family Chair of Leadership at Tyndale Seminary, Toronto, Ontario, Canada, 4.7.8-9). He is now associate dean of biblical and theological studies and professor of Christian ethics at Wheaton College.

27. Eugene Peterson, "Follow the Leader," *Fuller Focus*, Fall 2001, 31.

> The crucial need for true servanthood in the church today cannot be overemphasized, precisely because such a high premium has been put on a certain kind of strong, visionary leadership to change the church and turn it around. There is a certain danger to such an emphasis on strong leadership: It may not be founded on true servanthood and devoted discipleship that follows Jesus all the way. Strong leadership of the wrong kind, often based on secular CEO and business management models, can end up with much pride, self-sufficiency, and therefore sin. What the church needs in order to be transformed into an Acts 2 type of community of faith (Acts 2:42-47) is the presence of true servants of Jesus who are filled with the Spirit, manifesting his fruit of love, joy, peace, patience, kindness, goodness, faithfulness, gentleness, and self-control (Gal. 5:22, 23). The church needs servants who engage in true service rather than self-righteous service and who will lead when called by God to do so, with humility and grace, in prayerful consultation with a plurality of other fellow servants also called to lead, in order to have a vision for the church that is God's, and not a vision born of human ambition or wanting to be great or to do great things.[28]

"Strong leadership of the wrong kind, often based on secular CEO and business management models, can end up with much pride, self-sufficiency, and therefore sin."

It is therefore more biblically correct to say that Jesus Christ through the church is the hope of the world, and *servants* are the hope of the church.

28. Tan, *Full Service*, 137.

7 Serving through Wisdom

James E. Bradley

Editor's Introduction Once we establish that servanthood is an important aspect of pastoral ministry, the question emerges of what channels are available for us to serve others. In this essay James Bradley, who teaches church history at Fuller Theological Seminary, reminds us of a wise and venerable tradition of older pastors serving younger pastors by writing letters to them. In an era where pastoral training has become both contractual and institutional, highlighting this highly personal form of service expands our imagination by showing how pastoral wisdom can be passed on from one pastor to the next.

Before the seminary movement first offered postbaccalaureate theological education in the early decades of the nineteenth century, aspiring pastors were trained at universities and colleges alongside their colleagues in the other main professions of law and medicine.[1] Youthful graduates in divinity, fresh from the university, often found their first leadership experience as assistants to senior pastors, who served as "nursing fathers" and mentors in the ministry. This personal mentoring relationship in turn gave rise to a vast body of literature in the form of "letters of advice" to young ministers. Hence, before the first seminary in America was established at Andover in 1808, the accepted form of theological training embraced a mentoring model that assumed a close working relationship between established pastors and young, inexperienced

1. A full book-length study of this topic will appear shortly under the title *Spiritual Formation in Ministry: The Unity and Fragmentation of* Theologia, *1650-1900*.

ones. This pattern of training assumed that leadership had to do with wisdom acquired over time and through experience, but that the wisdom so attained could be articulated and handed down to future generations. The principles of leadership found in these letters of advice and the patterns of mentoring that produced them are the subject of this essay.

While the seminary movement aimed to remedy some of the inherent weaknesses in the mentoring method of education, and while it was eminently successful for most of the nineteenth century, regrettably the seminaries themselves eventually took the place of the earlier patterns. Later, under the influence of the universities and modern science, education for ministry increasingly privileged knowledge as "information" over knowledge as "wisdom." Hence, knowledge as science and power gradually usurped an older understanding of knowledge as wisdom and service, and by the early twentieth century letters of advice to young ministers had ceased to exist. Mentoring in ministry today is largely a lost art, and in this essay I wish not only to introduce this ancient way but possibly also to help provoke the recovery of its practice. It is my hope that the forming of mentoring relationships might serve the next generation of pastors through the accumulated wisdom of the past and might move us forward in the genuine renewal of theological education today.

Education for ministry increasingly privileged knowledge as "information" over knowledge as "wisdom."

In the early modern literature on Christian leadership, letters of advice from skilled, experienced pastors were written, often published, and handed down to the younger generation. Based in part on the book of Proverbs, the literature of formation for Christian leaders made a consistent connection between inner integrity and outward prudence, between virtue and discretion; in a word, the literature assumed that inner moral goodness, good judgment, and the work of the ministry are found together. The manuals for young ministers thus make several important assumptions: (1) that the practice of inward devotion to Christ was conducive to discretion, (2) that discretion, prudence, or wisdom could be taught, and (3) that discretion or wisdom was essential for effective ministry. While wisdom will indeed be attained throughout one's life, it may also be taught: in other words, it is possible to inculcate wise behavior. This behavior, in turn, was believed to lead to effective and faithful service in the church.

The inculcation of wisdom in young leaders was never thought to be easy, or always, in every case, successful, though it could be "managed." In fact, the entire subject was thought to be enormously difficult, as Presbyterian John Erskine said: "Likewise, in healing wounded consciences, in reconciling those at variance, in encouraging the disconsolate, in speaking to those on a death-bed, in managing the public business, and in exercising the discipline of the church; all their sagacity, caution, penetration and judgment, are little enough to choose out the properest means, and to apply them with dexterity, that they may not spoil the best designs by bad management."[2] The process of formation for ministry was also judged to be long and arduous. "An able minister of the New Testament," wrote John Collett Ryland, "is not formed in a day or a year; no, not in seven or ten years; happy is that young man, who arrives to any degree of maturity and strength of mind, in the compass of twenty years."[3] But while difficult, the effort these authors gave to exhortation and warning clearly suggests their belief that passing on the wisdom born of experience and admonishing young ministers to nurture discretion was a worthy endeavor and a key for the effective leadership of the future generation.

By examining a few illustrations of the kind of advice that was offered, we can see how wisdom was generated through long and varied ministerial experiences and how it was conferred through a close mentoring relationship. The common good of the community of faith, for example, was constantly in view in this literature. The good of the whole would arise from the minister striking a balance between two competing dispositions: first, "seriousness" with respect to the nature of the faith (for it deals with eternal truths), and second, "affection" or generous care for others based on God's care for us. This balanced disposition guided the minister in dealing with people in a wide range of matters. Naturally, advice clustered around areas of conflict in the community. In admonishing people for wrong or godless behavior, for example, ministers needed a serious approach to the misguided person, along with compassion for the person and a recognition of the minister's own accountability. When people who need to be rebuked, it was said, perceived that the ministers themselves

2. John Erskine, "The Qualifications Necessary for Teachers of Christianity" (1750), in *Discourses Preached on Several Occasions* (Edinburgh, 1798), 31-32.

3. John Collett Ryland, *Dr. Cotton Mather's Student and Preacher; or, Directions for a Candidate of the Ministry,* Walford edition (London, 1789), preface, vii-viii.

were ready to fall under the just condemnation of God, *then* they would feel and respond to the importance of the rebuke. "An affectionate manner insinuates itself with the heart, renders it soft and pliable, and disposes it to imbibe the sentiments and follow the impulse of the speaker."[4]

Similar considerations applied to situations where it was necessary to correct those who opposed sound teaching. When ministers were called to oppose wrong doctrine, the letters of advice commended a positive approach; do it by establishing the doctrine that others seek to destroy, it was said, and separate the real truth from the errors mingled with it.[5] The absence of "success" was handled similarly. To a discouraged younger Methodist minister whose "society" was losing members, Adam Clarke recommended copying Christ's conduct toward the seven churches in Asia. "Preface all that you have to say on the head of their backsliding, with the good that still remains in them; and make that *good* which they still possess, the reason why they should shake themselves from the dust, take courage, and earnestly strive for more." "I tried the former [haranguing way]," Clarke added, "and did no good: I abandoned it, and adopted the latter, and God blessed it."[6] In the end a clergyman is answerable for his fidelity and his diligence, and not for his "success."[7]

Guidance could be offered in the area of what *not* to do, as well as in areas of positive duty. Do not hinder success, said the evangelical Anglican Richard Cecil, "by being too sharp-sighted, too quick-eared, or too ready-tongued." "Some evils are irremediable: they are best neither seen nor heard: by SEEING and HEARING things which you cannot remove, you will create implacable adversaries; who, being guilty aggressors, never forgive." Never speak meanly or harshly of anyone, Cecil added.[8] Rules such as this seem to have arisen from long experi-

4. Robert Hall, *On the Discouragements and Supports of the Christian Minister. A Discourse Delivered to the Rev. James Robertson, at His Ordination . . .*, 7th ed. (London, 1824), 27.

5. Joseph Kinghorn, *Advice and Encouragement to Young Ministers: Two Sermons, Addressed Principally to the Students of the Two Baptist Academies, at Stepney and at Bristol* (Norwich, 1814), 2:31.

6. Adam Clarke, *A Letter to a Preacher, on His Entrance Into the Work of the Ministry: Containing Observations on the Most Important Discharge of the Ministerial Office*, 3rd ed. (London, 1812), 6.

7. Clarke, *Letter*, 6.

8. *The Works of the Rev. Richard Cecil*, ed. Josiah Pratt, 3 vols., 2nd ed. (London, 1816), 3:605.

ence, and they imparted an approach to human behavior that could not be found in textbooks of theology. Philip Doddridge, as well, in his work as tutor at Northampton Academy, had seen the terrible effects of an unbalanced temper that was too serious and lacked affection. "An unreasonable stiffness in little matters will do unspeakable mischief. I almost tremble to see it in any designed for the ministry. I foresee in it the confusion of congregations, and the ruin of your own character and usefulness."[9] James Coleridge, an Anglican priest, had arrived at the same conclusion, whether on his own or on the basis of the corporate wisdom: one should be cautious, said Coleridge, in forming an opinion of the characters of individuals in the parish, and still more cautious in expressing it. It was imperative to avoid premature scrutiny into the personal conduct of people; the knowledge thus gained, though possibly correct, would likely cause more damage to the reputation of the pastor than it was worth. "Time will gradually unfold to him much painful information on this head; and experience will enable him to make the proper use of it."[10]

The balance of seriousness and affection was particularly needed when visiting and caring for the sick and infirm.

Wisdom had to do preeminently with knowing people and their habits, both in the community and, in considerable depth, at the individual level. The balance of seriousness and affection was particularly needed when visiting and caring for the sick and infirm. "Great discretion is required in the right discharge of it [i.e., visitation]; for there may be danger in administering either too much *fear,* or too much hope." But superficiality in all its forms was to be studiously avoided. When counseling the afflicted, the wise minister must consider not only who asks but also what he or she asks: "no flattery is so fatal as that of the physician or the divine."[11] These illustrations are important for our purposes because they demonstrate the notion that wisdom in the practical matters of

9. Philip Doddridge, *Lectures on Preaching, and the Several Branches of the Ministerial Office* (London, 1821), 11.

10. James D. Coleridge, *Practical Advice to the Young Parish Priest* (London, 1834), 24.

11. Jeremy Taylor, *Rules and Advices to the Clergy of the Diocese of Down and Connor, for Their Deportment in Their Personal and Public Capacities,* 2nd ed. (London, 1663), 20, 26.

ministry emerged from much experience and could be communicated through a written account passed down from one generation to the next.

This selfless giving for the common good of the community was thought to derive in some sense from the personal integrity of the pastor. A constant theme in the letters of advice was the importance of the self-control of the minister, nurtured by the cardinal spiritual disciplines of prayer, study, meditation, and especially solitude. In each ministerial practice, wise and prudent action arose from personal integrity and good character. Such character, in turn, was formed by the exercise of spiritual disciplines, and both the prudence of the action and the discipline that nurtured it could be cultivated and deepened through wise council. Conversely, to suppose that wise action in the community could occur in ministerial practice apart from self-understanding, the exercise of spiritual disciplines, and good advice would have been considered the very definition of folly.

Paradoxically, the community was served best when pastors nurtured self-knowledge and self-transcendence through solitude. Solitude has to do with what George Herbert, renowned Anglican pastor of the seventeenth century, called the "Parson in Sentine." Here, while alone and quiet, the pastor "keeps God's watch" and everything comes under his test and censure.[12] This was such a crucial aspect of the formation of young ministers and the sustainability of their vocation that William Paley, the well-known ethicist, observed, "Were I required to comprise my advice to a young clergyman in one sentence it should be in this, learn to live alone." Solitude focused one's energies, it was "a preservative of character" and was even called the secret to happiness in the clerical vocation.[13] By far and away the most important function of solitude was self-knowledge. In solitude the principal goal, in Methodist Jonathan Edmondson's words, was "to acquire that knowledge of the internal man, which is absolutely necessary in the duty of self government."[14] Solitude was not merely seclusion, because in solitude the main idea was to adopt the habit of rigorous self-examination. Moreover, Paley too emphasized

12. George Herbert, *A Priest to the Temple, or the Country Parson, His Character, and Rule of Holy Life*, 2nd ed. (London, 1671), 60.

13. William Paley, *Advice Addressed to the Young Clergy of the Diocese of Carlisle in a Sermon Preached at a General Ordination . . .* (London, 1782), 24.

14. Jonathan Edmondson, *A Concise System of Self-government, in the Great Affairs of Life and Godliness, on Scriptural and Rational Principles* (London, 1816), 218.

the inner unity between the practice of solitude, the acquisition of self-knowledge, and the importance of self-transcendence.

Finally, integrity and self-transcendence in the minister were dialectically related to the good of the whole community. Indeed, attending to the needs of the community was one measure for testing genuine personal integrity, and the connection becomes obvious when we examine the minister's role in settling controversies. In the midst of resolving conflict, ministers must, above all, be reluctant to pronounce judgment. Pray for an erring person, pastors were advised, reprove him if necessary, but leave sentence to his judge.[15] Similar considerations apply with even more force when ministers themselves were provoked or criticized personally. "We shall hurt both our own cause and that of religion dreadfully, if we return it [criticism]: and do honour to both, if we behave under it calmly."[16] So ministers were encouraged to take time for cool deliberation; "be quick to retract, instead of eager to defend a mistake. — Make it appear, that it is no hard task for you to pronounce those little words, *I was mistaken.*"[17] How? The pastor should be more ready to suspect himself of ignorance, prejudice, or error than to fasten these charges on others. "Be careful so to order yourself, that you fall not into temptation and folly in the presence of any of your charges," especially intemperate chidings, or clamors, or scoldings. If you do, you are "likely to be lost from all possibility of receiving much good from your ministry."[18] In this advice we can almost hear the tone of voice of the elder, experienced pastor admonishing the younger. The ancient pattern of handing down wisdom from generation to generation, while it eventually led to a published "book," originally assumed a close, personal relationship between an elder mentor and a young person learning to be a Christian leader.

In the midst of resolving conflict, ministers must, above all, be reluctant to pronounce judgment.

Max De Pree's understanding of leadership is grounded in his belief

15. Taylor, *Rules,* 19.

16. Thomas Secker, *Eight Charges Delivered to the Clergy of the Dioceses of Oxford and Canterbury,* 2nd ed. (London, 1771), 272.

17. Thomas Wilson, *Hints to Young Ministers: Designed More Particularly for the Use of Those Educated at Hoxton Academy* (London, 1802), 10-11.

18. Taylor, *Rules,* 8.

that we are all made in the image of God and that we possess a diversity of gifts that are given for the common good. His convictions regarding the importance of respect for the individual person, human equality, and the larger good of the group lead directly to a particular shape, or ordering, of human relationships. Inner character is the foundation for effective leadership manifested outwardly in the community. Leaders, then, acting out of these convictions, will demonstrate their values in terms of their commitment to personal integrity, self-restraint, building relationships, and nurturing community. These values and this way of ordering human relations are fully congruent with the early modern understanding of leadership development in the manuals of pastoral advice.

Remarkably, the themes that emerge from this old literature are personal integrity, the importance of relationships, and the good of the community. It is almost as if Max himself had taken a page from the books of these early pastors and mentors, although it is more likely that both he and they had simply followed the yet more traveled path of an even more ancient book. Arguably, if we are to see genuine renewal in theological education in our present context, we may need to encourage young, aspiring pastors today to seek out the counsel of older, more experienced men and women in the ministry. Conversely, one of the most revered traditions in pastoral ministry is the privilege, unique to experienced and older pastors, of nurturing, guiding, and watching over the lives and ministries of young people. May this tradition of mentoring and this literature of pastoral advice stimulate the young to seek out older, wise mentors, and may it encourage experienced pastors to take a fresh initiative in the crucial task of guiding the young in the ways of Christian formation for ministry.

Arguably, if we are to see genuine renewal in theological education in our present context, we may need to encourage young, aspiring pastors today to seek out the counsel of older, more experienced men and women in the ministry.

8 Evaluating Servanthood: From Servant Leadership to Leading as Serving

David Augsburger

Editor's Introduction On one level, this notion of servanthood coming from the corporate world is an easy sell for those of us in pastoral ministry because, after all, isn't that what ministry is all about? The extolling of servanthood can seem more like an affirmation of our vocational identity than a challenge to which we should aspire. In this chapter David Augsburger, who teaches practical theology at Fuller Theological Seminary, challenges this assumption by questioning whether we are the best judge of our own servanthood. Augsburger claims that since people judge others' actions by their effects and their own actions by their intentions, we can learn much about our own servanthood by relying on others to help us make an evaluation.

To lead,
One must follow.
Fail to honor people,
They will fail to honor you.
A good leader talks little,
(Acts quietly, serves simply.)
When the work is done,
The aim fulfilled,
They will all say,
"We did this ourselves."

Lao Tzu

> *When Yen Ho was about to take up his duties as tutor to the heir of Ling, Duke of Wei, he went to Ch'u Po Yu for advice.*
>
> *"I have to deal with a man of depraved and murderous disposition," he said. "How is one to deal with a man of this sort?"*
>
> *"I am glad that you asked this question," said Ch'u Po Yu. "The first thing you must do is not to improve him, but to improve yourself."*
>
> Taoist story, China

Leadership is a "glow word" on many lips. Politicians pretend it. Youth question it. The old yearn for it. Parents grasp for it. Children defy it. Police seek it. Armies impose it. Terrorists seize it. Executives claim it. Corporations exploit it. Scholars study it. Pundits pretend it. Sound bites impose it. Media announce it. Sycophants worship it. Religions bless it. Psychologists psych it. Autocrats manipulate it. Experts teach it. Conservatives defend it. Liberals suspect it. Ethicists critique it. Philosophers debate it. Theologians integrate it. (Those who love it, one suspects, should rarely be granted it; those who usurp it not allowed it; those who feel entitled to it not be entrusted with it; only those who accept it as a trust — a service delegated by community and for community — deserve to serve in it.)

Servant leadership is an even more confusing and often confused concept. Leadership involves the ability to inspire and influence the thinking, attitudes, and behavior of people. Inspiring others to reach goals of common good — a service — is less frequent than influencing others to contribute to the leader's good — a common vice. Leadership, as the role with authority to exercise power, can be the opportunity for authentic service to all participants, or a selective service contributing to the few. In the last twenty years the concept of servant leadership has been used to correct the tendency toward misuse of authority, or abuse of position and power. It has been co-opted, a temptation leaders sometimes find it hard to resist, as a cover for motivations other than authentic service.

Not "Servant Leadership," but Leading as Serving

"Servant leadership" may contain a great range of motivations; leading that pursues serving others is more focused on a more sharply defined range of actions we can call "service." Swiss theologian Karl Barth wrote as a theology of service: "Service is a willing, working, and doing in which a person acts not according to his own purposes or plans but with a view to the purpose of another person and according to the need, disposition and direction of others. It is an act whose freedom is limited and determined by the other's freedom, an act whose glory becomes increasingly greater to the extent that the doer is not concerned about his own glory but about the glory of the other."[1] Leading as serving — service as the soul of leadership — requires that we explore the primary referent point of the leader in understanding both terms. The simplicity of the language that follows is not setting forth the elementary simplicity of "good, nice, unselfish behavior," refreshing as that is when we encounter it. It is seeking the simplicity that lies beyond the complexity of analysis, reflection, examination, rumination, research, and evaluation. The second simplicity that emerges after the labor-intensive analyses are completed is the distilled wisdom that moves us beyond naive service to authentic service that is constructive and transformative of frozen systems and fossilized practices and patterns.

The tendency to elevate position over function, being over doing and role over action, leads to the separation of person from behavior. The leader may be described as a fine upstanding responsible person who unfortunately is compelled by circumstances to make decisions of ambiguous ethics, design systems that may be unfortunately exploitive of some, carry out profitable but fatally flawed programs. This splitting of being from doing permits actions that would be unacceptable to the person in actual interpersonal relationships. In virtual relationships to the statistical digits that replace living employees, actions can be taken that end employment, wipe out pensions, impoverish families but solidify the company's profits and elevate stock values. "Servant leadership" can be *leadership that serves* when person and action become one, when means and end are united in an ethic of concern for the good of more than one, or the circles that surround one and guarantee safety and security.

1. Karl Barth, *Evangelical Theology: An Introduction* (Grand Rapids: Eerdmans, 1963), 184.

Egocentric Service versus Allo-centric Service

Service with self as the ultimate end (egocentric) narrows the criteria for success to what is good for me; service with the other as end (allo-centric) thinks in increasingly wider circles of influence and impact. In the language of the second simplicity, after the data has emerged from exhaustive analysis of variants, the service is about "me" or it is finally about "others."

Does authentic service arise from a compassion generated within? Or is it a compulsion fed by reinforcement and rewards that are earned from without? Is it a virtue or a utilitarian set of behaviors? Ethicist and philosopher Alasdair MacIntyre offers a definition of a virtue: "A virtue is an acquired human quality the possession and exercise of which tends to enable us to achieve those goods which are internal to practices and the lack of which effectively prevents us from achieving any such goods."[2] Service, as a practice that is motivated largely by external rewards, is not a virtue. Practices become virtues when they are motivated by rewards internal to the practice itself. Service comes in widely contrasting forms and types, from the nonvirtuous that is related to the baser motivations of greed, pride, and love of power to the more virtuous that seeks rewards distinct from compensation, competition, or domination.

After the data has emerged from exhaustive analysis of variants, the service is about "me" or it is finally about "others."

To visualize the contrasting varieties, we shall look at a continuum, a spread sheet, of service motivations. Six different types of service can be clarified by examining their essential, not their publicly stated, goals. Appropriate questions are: Is the service done primarily for the benefit of the server or the one served? Is the motive self-advancement, ego enhancement, or genuine concern for the other? These are not pejorative questions nor do they have illusive answers. Service and its benefits to the giver and the receiver are open, visible, self-evident to the recipient, the observer, and, if the actors are at all self-reflective, the "servant" as well.

Let us visualize a range of motivations for service. All six types of service are commonly seen in a day's work.

2. Alasdair C. MacIntyre, *After Virtue: A Study in Moral Theory* (Notre Dame, Ind.: University of Notre Dame Press, 1981), 178.

Motivations for Service Continuum

"It's really about me." — *"It's truly about you."*

Self-serving / other-using ←→ Other-serving / self-forgetting

1	2	3	4	5	6
Exploitive Service	**Egocentric Service**	**Equalitarian Service**	**Obedient Service**	**Benevolent Service**	**Sacrificial Service**
Service done solely for self-advancement, profit gained, righteousness demonstrated, moral superiority proved, power seized, political clout claimed.	Service that fulfills ego needs, that inflates self-esteem, that justifies one's pride, raises one above others, or claims virtue.	Service that is an equal benefit to both parties, a quid pro quo exchange of help and benefits of reward or repayment.	Service that fulfills a moral imperative to care for the neighbor, help the needy, even aid the enemy, out of a committed, willing obedience to a core of internalized values.	Service that is freely given, offered as a gift, that goes beyond mere payment. It is primarily offered out of caring, mercy, or compassion.	Service that is self-forgetting concern for the other's needs, that helps even though the cost requires real sacrifice and voluntary self-investment.

Primarily External Rewards — *Primarily Internal Rewards*

Egregious *egocentric* service is unmistakable in those eager for recognition, quick to do the visible, and unavailable for the invisible. Routine *equalitarian* service, the give-and-take exchanges of daily life, when done with civility and social responsibility, is the stuff of good business, good citizenship, good social judgment and behavior. *Obedient* service suggests that the person is responding to a higher standard than the "something exchanged for something" (quid pro quo) of routine transactions. This higher standard may be a principle of behavior of internalized values or simply obedient behavior in answer to inner parents. It may be obedience to a moral conscience or a sense of divine command to serve the neighbor. *Benevolent* service and *sacrificial* service answer to yet a higher call. Both arise from a deep commitment to act in love toward the neighbor, to serve out of concern or compassion for the other's needs, to offer help even at one's own expense because it believes that love is something you do, and participation in community requires doing more for others than expected, offering more than you have to do, may be asked to do, or would need to offer. *A spirituality of service calls one toward benevolent and sacrificial service.*

Some persons may consistently choose a single style of service, others are highly situational and utilitarian. A person may do an act that is egocentric followed by another that is benevolent. Public service may vary from exploitive machination with a public-relations spin to actual social concern for the good of fellow citizens. Effective leadership requires that one be able to clearly define oneself, one's role, one's position on central issues. This can be done in an egocentric self-presentation, in an equalitarian stance of mutuality, in a clearly defined principled position, in an altruistic commitment to the good of each and all in the organization with loyalty and security affirmed, or it can exemplify a willingness to forgo some significant personal profit for the welfare of others, to contribute sacrificially to what is just and right in both policy and practice. Leadership that is shaped by higher motivations of service hears the call to work toward the goal of humanitarian, compassionate, common welfare action in administration.

Questions for Measurement of Service Motives

In any human transaction, one discovers upon reflection, the actor judges the virtue of the action by the intentions; the recipient evaluates it by the consequences. Self-evaluations are inevitably biased by the inner assessment of laudable goals; the onlooker's summation, in contrast, is more often based on the visible results. Self-report questionnaires are inevitably biased by intentions taking precedence over actions, influence and outcomes being inflated by personal issues of esteem and regard, and many consider them of questionable value. The real test of any person's behavior is the impact of the server on those observing or those receiving the service. They alone can judge the authenticity of the action without justifying it with good intentions or gilding it with sterling motivations. It is possible to elicit feedback from associates, from those above in the chain of command, from peers in parallel positions, or from those beneath in the organizational structure, if the climate for such conversations is set in a context of mutual and supportive growth. As a starting point, the following questionnaire is useful for feedback from (a) a spouse, (b) a counselor/spiritual director, (c) a growth group in which a climate of self-disclosure and honesty is present, (d) selected observers interviewed by a neutral third party as a part of an evaluation process, (e) close friends who know one's inner life, (f) an opponent who has felt the heat of struggle and opposition in serious differences that have or have not been resolved. A peer group, or selected cotravelers invited to offer feedback on patterns of behavior, can provide a reality principle for a leader who otherwise receives only self-serving feedback from advancing subordinates or competitive commentary from colleagues and coworkers. If the faculty served by a dean, the staff served by a supervisor, the team administrated by an executive is invited to offer a measure of a person's central tendencies, some degree of clarity is possible, some measure of honesty in reflection and evaluation. If none of the above appear appropriate to the work situation, and so are not attempted, at least reading and answering the items with one other trustworthy and candid person will simulate the threat of such a process and may stimulate honest self-evaluation. (Nothing clears the mind as well as the thought of approaching death or a confrontation with truth.)

Motivations for Service Questionnaire

(To be filled out by witnesses to the leader desiring self-evaluation. The leader may do a self-rating to compare with the observers.)

1. In ________'s service, the external rewards are obvious, and effective service is designed to result in his/her personal advancement or success.
2. In ________'s service, the personal satisfaction and fulfillment of ego needs — identity justified, worth confirmed, dignity praised — are clearly seen.
3. In ________'s service, there is an evenhandedness, a fairness, a give-and-take, a quid pro quo that is always visible.
4. In ________'s service, there is a sense that she/he acts according to a higher law, a principled set of values that directs what is done.
5. In ________'s service, the unique characteristic is uncalculating generosity that goes beyond profit or payback.
6. In ________'s service, the main thing noticed is a compassionate willingness to offer aid in situations of need and unstrategic concern for the other's welfare.
7. In ________'s service, there is always a payoff, and ________'s stories invariably end in personal triumph.
8. In ________'s service, personal pride in being able to help others is of paramount importance.
9. In ________'s service, there is a give-and-take, a mutuality of reward that offers gratification to the one who serves as well as gratitude in the one served.
10. In ________'s service, one recognizes that although the person is important, the real issue is what is right, what is fair, what is the good thing to do.
11. In ________'s service, it is the uncalculated compassion, the genuine kindness that stands out in what is done.
12. In ________'s service, the fact that it may require sacrifice, or be costly to self, schedule, resources, or energy, is not an obstacle to service.

(Items 1-6 and 7-12 are parallel; i.e., items 1 and 7 are drawn from the first position on the scale, 6 and 12 from the last, and so forth.)

Extraordinary Service

Extraordinary people serve others for the others' sake, not for their own. We have every right to expect such service from each of the professions: for example, that the medications my physician prescribes will not be chosen by virtue of the free meals and the fringe benefits given by the drug companies; that the care physicians provide will not be solely for the fees received; that the decisions they make will not be dictated by the policies or profits of the HMO. We must be able to trust that the ethics of those practicing medicine define a service that is centered in the welfare of the patient — especially if we are the patient or have any influence on how health care is given to those we serve.

Self-giving service is more often the product of personal character, not a professional code of ethics.

We expect that the help we receive from a pastor, a therapist, an attorney, a financial adviser, an investment counselor, a bank officer, a policeman — to begin a long list of professions — will be unbiased, disinterested, eminently fair, genuinely altruistic service. We know that this is not always the case, so we look for certification that vouches for the quality of service given. Our expectation is that it will be at minimum, level three, truly equalitarian respect that is committed to the practice of equal justice.

However, self-giving service is more often the product of personal character, not a professional code of ethics. Each of us seeks trustworthy persons whose service is not primarily to their own advantage. We want service that is truly about the one being served. We feel the warmth of surprise when another goes beyond the social minimum or the professional norm to offer benevolent care, or sacrificial service that is not convenient, not routine, not the standard.

The step from self-service to mutuality, from self-advancement to equality, from self-profit to reciprocity is a great step upward in human relationships. It is not only the basis for fairness in the practice of service, and justice in the business of service, it is also the foundation of fair and equal economic community.

Some leaders get such enjoyment out of what they are able to do in joint service with their collaborators that they throw themselves into it with abandon. Self-forgetfully they see the task as greater than any one person's ego or agenda. They may push and cajole, nudge and prod to reach goals. Their style or character may not be studied or conscientious, and they may spend little time in self-evaluation or reflection. But their central motivation rises from that highest form of love, the love beyond *agape* called in the New Testament *koinonia.* They get intense rewards out of completing a task, or seeing others achieve their goals. This too is service, service to *others,* service reaching beyond the self.

Service: When Worship and Work Become One

Spirituality and service are sometimes viewed as direct opposites. Spirituality is detached from the tasks of life; service is engagement with the mundane, the routine, the earthly, the material. The spiritual, in contrast to these daily tasks of caring and giving care, is seen reaching toward the transcendent, the ineffable, the heavenly.

These should be reversed. Service, in more thoughtful theological reflection, is akin to worship. Indeed, in the Greek of the New Testament texts, service and worship are the same word. Spirituality is best seen in how one responds to the neighbor, to the face of actual human need.

It is important to end any reflection on service by reiterating that it is a recurring theme, a central and self-defining theme in the teaching of Jesus. Service was the essential virtue he prized and practiced. Those who participate in the community that surrounds and follows Jesus, recognize that the call to service is the call to discipleship. No one follows Jesus except by welcoming a life of service. He was the one who lived to serve others without regard for the cost. If Jesus was the man who lived to serve others, Dietrich Bonhoeffer argued, then it follows that the church is only the church when it exists for others in the practice of *agape.*

Those who participate in the community that surrounds and follows Jesus, recognize that the call to service is the call to discipleship.

This *agapaic* love, he noted, results in three kinds of service: (1) the service of listening to others that is a living extension and expression of the work of God, the Great Listener; (2) the service of active helpfulness in the bothersome things of life, the little irritations that offer us an opportunity to be interrupted by God and respond to none other than God; and (3) the service of forbearance where the strong help the weak, the healthy the ill, the righteous the fallen. In Christian forbearance we are drawn together toward God. "Nobody is too good for the meanest service. One who worries about the loss of time that such petty, outward acts of helpfulness entail is usually taking the importance of his own career too solemnly."[3]

Following Jesus is joining in the service of humanity made particular in the service of the actual individual sister or brother. Undeniable in his teaching and demonstrated in his life are the recurrent themes of the necessity and dignity of service.

Greatness is found in service, not dominance
(Mark 10:44; Luke 22:25-26).
Seek not to be great, seek to be a servant.

Leadership is offered in serving, not commanding
(Mark 10:44; Matt. 20:25).
To serve is to lead, to lead is to serve.

Vocation is discovered in serving, not being served
(Mark 10:45; Luke 22:27).
Caring is our calling.

Motivation is worthy in serving God, not greed, gain, or gold
(Luke 16:13; Matt. 6:24).
A soul sold for gold is a soul lost.

Discipleship is self-forgetful sacrificial service
(John 12:24-26).
"It is in giving that we receive, in losing life that we find it."

Simplicity in serving the innocent is serving God
(Mark 9:36-37).
See a child, serve a child, you serve God.

Authority is integrity, humility, charity, not rank
(Matt. 23:11; Luke 22:24-27).
Service nourishes humility, dominance feeds arrogance.

3. Dietrich Bonhoeffer, *Life Together,* trans. John W. Doberstein (New York: Harper and Row, 1954), 96-99.

9 Spiritual Formation as Service: The Essential Foundation for Leadership

Richard Peace

Editor's Introduction Once we've established that servanthood is an important but often elusive goal, the question becomes how one develops a servant's heart. Is it simply a matter of setting a goal and then working toward it, or is something else involved? In this chapter Richard Peace, who teaches theology at Fuller Theological Seminary, makes a case for the importance of spiritual formation in the life of a pastor. Jesus' own life and ministry were shaped by spiritual formation, and pastors would do well to emulate his model.

Who you are is how you lead. It is that simple — and that difficult. If leadership were merely a mechanical process — feed in the data, compare it to past situations, and come up with the best way forward — a computer could be built to do it. (Think how much cheaper a computer would be than the salary of a CEO!) But leadership is far more complex and far less straightforward. It takes a human being (or a group of human beings) in the context of a community of interested parties to forge the best next step.

And in this process, character matters. The decisions one makes as a leader emerge out of a matrix of *inner* realities: one's professional training, past experience in similar situations, external constraints, expectations of stakeholders, and the core values of the leader. It is the issue of core values that I wish to address.

It is as we pay attention to the spiritual world that our core values are formed, shaped, developed, and honed ever more closely to the values of Jesus.

I want to argue that ongoing spiritual formation is vital for a leader.[1] It is as we pay attention to the spiritual world that our core values are formed, shaped, developed, and honed ever more closely to the values of Jesus. Core values are all about those deep inner realities that define the essence of who we are.

So, for example, for those of us who call ourselves Christians, a core value would be the Great Commandment to love. We are called upon to love God in a wholehearted, all-encompassing sort of way. And we are also called upon to love others with *agape* love, which is a kind of love-in-action regardless of what we may feel. But it is one thing to affirm this value; it is another for that value to become so central to who we are that we act instinctively in this fashion. How do we become the kind of people who not only affirm the Great Commandment but also are fully shaped by it?

This is what spiritual formation is all about: the ongoing process whereby we open ourselves to God and to the way of God so that over time we are shaped by God. Our core values emerge out of this ongoing encounter with God.

Spiritual formation is all about putting ourselves in those places where we are most apt to encounter God. Spiritual formation is all about engaging in those practices that help translate our Christian ideas into reflexive action in our daily life. Spiritual formation is all about seeking to be ever more closely conformed to the image of Jesus. The kind of person we become, over time as we engage in spiritual formation, enables us to be not just competent leaders but leaders who lead from a thoroughly Christian worldview.

The kind of person we become, over time as we engage in spiritual formation, enables us to be not just competent leaders but leaders who lead from a thoroughly Christian worldview.

Here is an example of the impact of ongoing spiritual formation. We have a new minister in our church. I do not know him well, but in just the short time that he has been our pastor I have sensed that he is leading

1. Actually, I would argue that ongoing spiritual formation is vital for everyone. Attention to the spiritual world in which we live is crucial lest we be overwhelmed and overdetermined by the natural world that is so present to us. We need to learn to listen to the still, small voice of God so as to become all God calls us to be.

out of a vital relationship with God. Sure, he has all the professional skills a pastor needs. He knows how to prepare a sermon. He has a good sense of liturgy. He is warm, outgoing, and engaging — the kind of person you would turn to in times of crises. But there is something underneath all that professional skill and experience. He is reflecting something (or better still, someone) deep within him. He is ministering out of his ongoing encounter with God. It is this formational factor that makes his ministry not just competent but spirit-enhanced.

I want to think with you about how our spiritual life forms us and forms our values and hence shapes our leadership, whether it be in ministry, the home, or a career. To this end I want to do an extended case study. I want to look at how Jesus was prepared by God for his ministry.[2] I think the challenges Jesus had to face and the equipping that came from God raise the very questions we need to confront as men and women who desire to be effective leaders. After this case study I will end by describing a way to access this kind of material in our ongoing formation, based on *The Spiritual Exercises* of Saint Ignatius.

The Preparation of Jesus for Ministry

How was Jesus prepared for his ministry? Even asking this question sounds odd. Jesus was the Son of God. As such he brought unique DNA to the whole process of ministry. He could draw upon perspectives and realities unavailable to anyone else. But still, Scripture talks about Jesus not just as divine but also as human. And as a human being he grew from childhood to adulthood, and in the process he learned vari-

2. I admit to being wary of seeing Jesus through a particular lens since there is a history of making Jesus into our own image. For example, in his 1925 book *The Man Nobody Knows,* businessman Bruce Barton portrays Jesus as a salesman, publicist, and role model for the "modern businessman." And in a more recent example, Laurie Beth Jones has written a book entitled *Jesus CEO* (Westport, Conn.: Hyperion, 1996). Jones, a management consultant, draws on the leadership techniques of Jesus Christ to provide tips on how to inspire and manage others. My own stance is that Jesus must be allowed to be Jesus and must be understood in his own context. Hence I will make extended comments on the baptism and temptation of Jesus as found in Matt. 3:13–4:11 before trying to glean some applications to the whole question of leadership and spiritual formation.

ous skills (such as driving a nail), he lived in a community (and so learned how to negotiate life with siblings and others), and he developed physically over time. I do not think it out of order to suggest that he underwent preparation for ministry.

Following his baptism, Jesus is led into the wilderness for a forty-day fast, during which he confronts the key issues of ministry. These two events that take place at the start of Jesus' ministry serve to focus his ministry.

I want to argue that in his baptism and subsequent temptation in the wilderness *Jesus was given all he needed for ministry.* Also, that in these two experiences he *confronted the key issues that had the power to undo his ministry.*

For thirty years Jesus lived, as far as we know, quite an ordinary life in a peasant village in Israel. During these so-called hidden years he most likely worked as an artisan/carpenter with his father Joseph. He learned Torah from the local rabbi. He participated in the religious and social events of his community.

But clearly he had, from an early age, a sense of his mission. In the one glimpse we have of Jesus as a twelve-year-old, after his anxious parents journey back to Jerusalem and find him in conversation with the teachers in the temple, he seems surprised that they were worried about him. "Did you not know that I must be in my Father's house?" (Luke 2:49).

At about age thirty he leaves Nazareth and journeys to the river Jordan to be baptized by his cousin John. Following his baptism, Jesus is led into the wilderness for a forty-day fast, during which he confronts the key issues of ministry. These two events that take place at the start of Jesus' ministry serve to focus his ministry.

The Baptism of Jesus

It all begins with his baptism. Let me single out three important elements in the baptism of Jesus that define and enable his ministry: the meaning of his baptism itself, his empowerment by the Holy Spirit, and the affirmation and blessing by God.

First, by choosing to be baptized ("John would have prevented him, saying, 'I need to be baptized by you'" [Matt. 3:14]) Jesus identifies with those he will seek, serve, and ultimately save. John is preaching a baptism of repentance, but Jesus has lived a sinless life and so has nothing to repent of. Rather, by his baptism Jesus identifies himself with the people of Israel, and in particular with their sins (and through them with the sins of the world), prefiguring his death for those sins. By this act he announces to whom he will minister and the core issue he will confront, and he does so in a way that connects him to the deepest of their needs.

Second, the Holy Spirit descends upon Jesus. The text says "like a dove." We do not know what this means. Clearly the word "like" signals that this is a simile, but we are so far removed from the event that it is hard to know just what such a simile would have conjured up in the minds of first-century readers. But the main point is clear. Jesus was empowered for ministry. He is not alone. It will not be up to him, unaided, to do the will of his Father in the world. There is a new inner reality of some sort; a new kind of relationship upon which he can draw.

Third, a voice from heaven declares: "This is my Son, the Beloved, with whom I am well pleased" (Matt. 3:17). The nature of this commendation is important to note. Jesus' identity is declared. He is the Son of God. There is conjecture on whether Jesus knew fully who he was prior to this declaration. No matter what the case might be, at this point there is no doubt. He knows his identity and thus his calling and destiny. His ministry emerges out of this reality. Furthermore, Jesus is affirmed. God the Father is well pleased with him. As he starts his ministry, Jesus does so with the strong blessing of God.

And so the Trinity is complete: Father, Son, Holy Spirit, together, one yet separate, the divine mystery is active at this special moment in time.

The connections to what we need as leaders about to embark on new ministries, new ventures, or new callings are almost too obvious to point out. What a clear-sighted, focused ministry we would have if it arises out of:

- *Identification* with the people with whom we will work, with their needs, interests, and issues. Such identification stands in sharp contrast to other motives for work or ministry: self-interest, our own needs and desires, the wish for affirmation, using people to meet our goals or the goals of a corporation. So the question becomes: What is our stance toward those we lead, serve, sell to, interact with, and work with? Jesus was so identified with the needs of his people that he was willing to die for them. This is an impossibly high standard for us, but it does point us in the right direction.

- *Empowerment* from within and from beyond. Sure, it is vital to be well trained, knowledgeable, and experienced, but we are still left with our limitations. This is just the nature of our human condition. We get tired, we fail to see crucial factors, we make bad decisions, we make self-serving decisions, we are at the wrong place at the wrong time, etc. We need all the help we can get. This help comes from within and without. From within, when we are in touch with our genuine feelings, deep motives, true calling, and unconscious reality, we are able to live a more integrated life. Such an integrated life brings with it energy, wisdom, and authenticity — all of which we need in order to lead. From without, well, the Holy Spirit is still active in the world, a gift from God, a gift of God, an empowering force that takes our meager offerings and multiplies their impact beyond recognition.

When we are in touch with our genuine feelings, deep motives, true calling, and unconscious reality, we are able to live a more integrated life. Such an integrated life brings with it energy, wisdom, and authenticity — all of which we need in order to lead.

- *Identity and affirmation.* We need to know who we are to activate our gifts, skills, and calling. With a strong sense of self — which includes knowing where we have come from and whose family we are part of — we can go into situations and not be threatened or diminished by the forces that come against us. And if identity gives us the base from which we operate, affirmation gives us the energy to keep going. When we know that he or she who has given us birth and life finds us to be wonderful, this blessing empowers far more than we can imagine.

What a powerful grid this provides for leaders to assess their own motives and vision as they begin a new ministry, a new company, or a new job.

The Temptation of Jesus

And so on this gloriously high note of an empowering encounter with God, the very next thing that Jesus must do is to go off into the stark, forbidding Judean wilderness for a forty-day fast. His preparation involves not just epiphanies and infilling but also desolation and challenge.

Jesus meets the devil in the wilderness. This was, apparently, the purpose of this forty-day sojourn. The devil comes at the end of the fast when he is "famished" (Matt. 4:1) — not the best possible situation. Jesus has reached the limits of human existence, and it is then that he must face the three temptations that will shape who he becomes. We have to believe that these are real temptations for Jesus and not just a sort of morality play in which we know the hero will brush aside these faint jabs of his enemy.

The first temptation has to do with food, of course. Jesus is famished. From reports out of prisoner of war camps we know that after a while all you think about is food — not success or power or even sex, only food. "Turn these stones into bread." Plenty of stones. What is wrong with using his power to meet his pressing need?

But, of course, this temptation is not just about bread. The challenge to turn stone to bread is preceded by the deeper challenge: "If you are the Son of God . . ." This is the real issue. Jesus was declared to be the beloved Son at his baptism, but now, forty hard days later, how could this be true? How presumptive! The whole question of his identity is raised. Will Jesus own who he is? This is central to his mission.

So why not prove that he is who he has been declared to be? "If you really want to know that this is true, do something that only the Son of God could do. You need bread. You have power to make bread — or do you actually have any power? Are you really the Son of God? If so, show me. No one could ever fault you for doing this: creating bread by which to break your fast and give you energy."

Jesus answers with a quotation from Deuteronomy 8:3. In its original context the statement that "one does not live by bread alone, but by every word that comes from the mouth of God" is about the forty years that Israel wandered in the desert and the manna that God gave them when they were hungry. During the forty years the people of Israel were tested, tried, and humbled as God sought to know what was truly in their hearts. Hunger, too, was part of their test. Would they really keep the commandments? Would they be God's special people in the world, a light to others, a demonstration of what God wanted to do in the world? Or would they use their "chosen-ness" for their own ends?

No, Jesus will not use his power for his own ends or even for his own needs. "One does not live by bread alone." So he will say no to his famished state. Instead, he will abide by the promises of God — to "every word that comes from the mouth of God." Jesus has just heard a word from the mouth of God. That word declared him to be the beloved Son. He will own that reality. He has no need to prove that what God said is true.

The whole question of materialism is lurking in the background of the first temptation. Will Jesus use his power to satisfy his material needs? It does not matter that these needs are legitimate or that no one would be harmed or disadvantaged if he turned a few stones into bread. Jesus refuses to use his power for ends not intended. His firmness during the first temptation sets the pattern for the rest of his ministry. He did no miracle that served him and his needs.

The second temptation moves on to new ground. The devil takes Jesus to the pinnacle of the temple in Jerusalem. This is the very heart of the city and center of the faith of Israel. "So you want to start a new religious movement? Well, here is the place to do it. Throw yourself off the pinnacle. You know what will happen. The angels will catch you. No harm will come to you. Hey, it says so in the Bible." (If Jesus wants to quote Scripture at him, well, the devil can quote Scripture right back at Jesus.) "And think about the spectacle. Everyone will know you are the Son of God. Your ministry will be off to a flying start!"[3]

Jesus can choose recognition, honor, a special place, a special ministry if he wants. Why stay in obscurity, on the margins of society? Would it not be better to start at the center, to be recognized for who he really is? Think of how much good could be done from this high-profile position.

Again Jesus answers from Deuteronomy. (In fact, all three of his responses will come from Deuteronomy 6–8.) This time his response/quotation is quite direct. "Do not put the Lord your God to the test." Of course the angels would protect him. Once again the temptation begins with the phrase "if you are the Son of God." Apparently this whole issue of self-doubt is a real temptation for Jesus. But even more, such a bizarre self-serving display of special power and place is not the way God has chosen to work. This is not God's way. This is not the mission of Jesus. Recognition is not his way. (Interestingly, hereafter Jesus goes out of his way to hide his power, for example, urging those he has healed to tell no one. The so-called messianic secret is a key theme in the Gospel of Mark.)

3. Sorry, I could not resist the pun.

The third temptation brings up the issue of power. The devil now takes Jesus to "a very high mountain" and offers him "all the kingdoms of the world and their splendor." Presumably the devil can make good on this offer, which gives us an interesting insight into the "principalities and powers" behind world systems. In other words, he is saying to Jesus, "You can become King of the World. Think how much good you can do with all that power. And why bother with the cross? It can be all yours now."

Jesus responds, again from Deuteronomy: "Worship the Lord your God, and serve only him." Presumably, if Satan is able to offer Jesus the world, Satan would remain the power behind the world system and thus Jesus would give Satan the "worship" due only God. Now Jesus banishes the devil with a word and he leaves and it is all over. Suddenly the angels appear. The temptation is finished. They minister to Jesus. And Jesus begins his ministry in Galilee.

For Jesus the easy path is the path pointed out to him by the devil. Use his power to satisfy his needs and the needs of others. Be recognized for who you really are and work from that place of honor. Seize power. It is yours to take and use. But this is not the path God would have him take.

Again, the connections to the call to leadership are obvious.

- *Meeting the devil:* The devil comes in many guises, even at times as an angel of light. The first task is to name the devil. What tempts us, challenges us, calls who we are into question? Is it our flawed self-image that gives room for the negative to speak? Our unnamed desires? Our unnoticed needs? We will be tempted, of this there is no doubt. But will we recognize this as temptation when it comes? Is our moral compass firmly in place so that we will be able to choose the "best way" over against the "good way," much less the "easy way"?
- *Owning our identity:* When times get tough we doubt our calling, our ability, our mission. What was clear in the light should not be doubted in the darkness. Moving back from our true identity will sabotage our mission.
- *Materialism:* Will we use our calling and mission to serve our own needs and ends? Will it be riches that motivate our mission or calling? Will it be reward (even legitimate reward) that makes the job worthwhile? Or is it faithfulness to our calling that is key?
- *Honor:* Do we labor so as to be recognized and honored? Is "being thought well of by others" what drives us?

- *Power:* Is this what we crave? Many do. Many find the path to power through work, mission, or ministry.

The desire for riches, honor, or power each has the ability to do in our otherwise worthwhile mission in life, as does the failure to recognize our temptations and name them for what they are or the inability to own who we are and what we are called to be and do.

Spiritual Formation

But how do we access all this for our own lives as leaders? It is one thing to notice the beginning of Jesus' ministry and to see the connections to our own lives. It is another to make these insights our own. How do we do this?

I want to suggest a way of formation, drawn from *The Spiritual Exercises* of Saint Ignatius. I draw upon Ignatius for several reasons. For one thing, I have found the way of Ignatius to be personally powerful for me in my own life over the last decade. I know this works. Second, the spiritual exercises have served as powerful formational tools for ministry for hundreds of years. This is a proven way of formation. Third, I think the way of Ignatius newly resonates with our cultural circumstances. As we move ever more deeply into a postmodern mind-set, away from the purely rational and into the world of imagination, art, and community, Ignatius gives us the tools to activate the right-brain way of imagination and story while at the same time honoring our left-brain rational processes.

Retreats

First, a word about time and place for spiritual formation. It is all well and good for us as followers of Jesus to have a regular time of Bible study, reflection, prayer, and meditation each day. This is foundational to our ongoing formation as Christians. But I have come to believe that we also need times away, in retreat, characterized by silence, worship, and focused reflection. Most of us do not have enough silence in our lives. Most of us have little time for active reflection on the things that matter. So we have to carve out times of retreat. At first it seems impossible to find a whole morning to spend at a retreat center. But when we do, we find that a morning is not enough. We need a whole day and then a whole weekend. Perhaps, in time, we can do an eight-day retreat or even a thirty-day retreat. Remember that it was during the forty days in the silence and solitude of the desert that Jesus faced his own deepest temptations and found the insight and strength to resist. This is not accidental. We too need time in the desert.

It is on retreat that we encounter God deeply. This gives us the base from which to draw in our daily reflections. And by retreat I do not mean the activist, word-filled, speaker-oriented retreats common in Protestant circles. Such retreats are of value, but we need more silent retreats in which we can learn to listen to God.

But how can busy leaders find such chunks of time in their schedules? Well, I would argue that we do find time for professional seminars, business conferences, and other multiday events. And once we have experienced the shaping power of retreat, we find that retreats are not an option but a necessity. Who we are is how we lead, and in retreat we have time and space to work at the question of who we are as followers of Jesus.

Ignatian Contemplation

What do we do on such retreats? Here is where Ignatian contemplation comes in. Saint Ignatius developed a variety of ways to pray.[4] One of the most useful methods is something he called *contemplation*.[5] The process is simple. Go to a gospel passage (or other narrative). Read through the text several times. Take notes on what you see and hear. What questions do you have about the passage? Think about what the passage means. Consult a commentary if you wish but only after you are thoroughly familiar with the passage. And go to the commentary with questions to which you need answers (e.g., about a particular cultural custom men-

4. Actually, Ignatius did not claim to be an innovator when it comes to prayer and spiritual practices. He adopted and adapted various methods already in use. However, it is in the very adaptation that his own innovation is found.

5. In fact, what Ignatius suggests is a form of meditation, not contemplation. Meditation is active reflection (which is what he is urging), whereas contemplation is usually described as a state of passive openness to the moment and to how God will fill it.

tioned in the passage, such as the use of water in first-century Jewish religious practices and its relationship to the baptism ritual by John). Use the commentary. Do not let it use you.

Then enter into the passage with your *imagination.* This is the distinctive part of Ignatian contemplation. Close your eyes. Consciously relax. Let your breathing slow down. Ask the Holy Spirit to guide your meditation. Then begin to imagine the scene you have read about. What was the wilderness of Judea like where Jesus went after his baptism? What did it look like? Smell like? Feel like? Imagine that you are there with Jesus, weary day after weary day with only water and little or no food to eat. Be with him when the devil comes. You are an unnoticed bystander. Listen to the temptations as they unfold. Enter into the temptations. As they are presented to you, what do they sound like? Which temptation resonates most deeply with you? Riches? Fame? Power? How do these temptations come to you in your own life?

- If your temptation is riches, how is this desire expressed in your life? How do you resist it? How do you give in to it? How much does it control what you do, the decisions you make, and the life you lead? What is God saying to you about riches?
- If your temptation is fame, how is this desire expressed in your life? How do you resist it? How do you give in to it? How much does it control what you do, the decisions you make, and the life you lead? What is God saying to you about your need to be recognized and honored?
- If your temptation is power, how is this desire expressed in your life? How do you resist it? How do you give in to it? How much does it control what you do, the decisions you make, and the life you lead? What is God saying to you about power and control?

Ignatian prayer has three parts to it: preparation, prayer, and review of prayer. In Ignatian contemplation the preparation is the Bible study you do as you get ready to enter into the world of the text. The prayer is the imaginative entering into the scene or the event and the listening to what is being said to you. The review of prayer is stepping back from the prayer and considering the whole experience. What did you learn? What did you hear? What did you feel? (Ignatius was particularly concerned that we get in touch with our feeling states, as these give valuable clues to what the Spirit is seeking to say to us.) How were you aware of God's presence? What issues did this time of prayer raise that you should consider in your next time of prayer?

By the way, a journal is vital to spiritual formation. You need to write down what you hear, see, and feel. You need to capture the whole experience in words so that you can continue to process it. A journal is especially necessary for review of prayer.

This kind of imaginative exercise forces us to consider who we are, how we live life, what motivates us, and what it means in actuality to follow Jesus in our ministry, mission, job, or business.

I use the example of Jesus' baptism and temptation because these raise issues that relate directly to those in leadership. The same process can be followed with any story from the life of Jesus. In this way we can make real our commitment to Jesus. Thus we allow ourselves to continue the process of being formed ever more closely to the image of Jesus. And as our core values grow more in accord with the image of Christ, so too our leadership evolves. Who we are is how we lead. May we, indeed, lead from the way of Christ.

10 The Service of Personal Identity: Created for "Good" Work

Linda Wagener

Editor's Introduction Is servanthood something we put on for our pastoral role but then take off again in other contexts? Although few pastors would actually frame the question in that way, often our behavior reveals some discontinuities between our professional and personal identities. In this chapter Linda Wagener, who teaches in the School of Psychology at Fuller Theological Seminary, challenges the modern notion that we can put on a set of values for our professional life that are not part of our personal identity. By this reasoning, one thing we can do to be better servants is to strive toward a better integration between personal and professional life.

> *"For many of us who work, there exists an exasperating discontinuity between how we see ourselves as persons and how we see ourselves as workers. We need to eliminate that sense of discontinuity and to restore a sense of coherence in our lives."*
>
> Max De Pree, *Leadership Is an Art*[1]

Let me invite you to take a moment to reflect on the central question of this chapter. Who are you? You will no doubt quickly find that you have multiple answers to this question, for indeed we have multiple identities. There are those associated with our workplace, for example, job titles or professional field. We have multiple identities within our family unit:

1. Max De Pree, *Leadership Is an Art* (New York: Doubleday, 1989), 32.

spouse, parent, child, sibling. We also have those identities that fill out our personalities: extrovert or introvert, driven or laid-back. Added to these are various aspects of the self that may situate us geographically, culturally, religiously, and recreationally.

As a further step in this thought exercise, picture yourself in your place of employment. By what standard do you measure the worth of your contribution? Even the phrase "good work" may have dual meaning. On the one hand it means good performance and is probably measurable as profit, production, growth, or achievement. On the other hand it refers to work that is ethical, meaning that it can be measured by the extent that it demonstrates contribution, compassion, caring, and commitment.

By what standard do you measure the worth of your contribution?

Divided Self

The postmodern context in which we live has geometrically increased the multiple identities that we need to integrate to have a coherent sense of self.[2] If I think about my day, which is probably similar to yours, I will be engaged in multiple contexts and relationships in which I will play varied roles in response to a range of expectations. I will begin and end my day as a householder, spouse, and parent. In between I will be an administrator, teacher, evaluator, supervisor, consultant, writer, therapist, mentor, colleague, consumer, and friend. I will have face-to-face contact with dozens of people who have varied expectations for our interaction. Finally I will have indirect contact by phone and e-mail with another set of people the size of a small village. All this can and usually does run fairly smoothly because we human beings are capable of flexibility and adaptation. We are good at responding to the contextual cues that shape "appropriate" behavior. We can "shift" our manners, language, dress, and *even our values* to match the culture of a context. And yet this ease of adaptation can lead to inconsistency, even hypocrisy.

2. Kenneth Gergen, *The Saturated Self: Dilemmas of Identity in Contemporary Life* (New York: Basic Books, 1991).

Under these conditions, developing an integrated personal identity becomes a crucial task. When the personal and public identities of people are split, as they often are in modern culture, we may function with multiple sets of values. Personal values are typically applied to personal, family, and religious life while public values are applied in the work setting. Instrumental competencies — our productivity, achievements, and skills — become part of our workplace identity while religious and moral values are frequently relegated to the private sphere. As a result, it has become acceptable and even normative for individuals to have one framework for "good work" and another for "good person." At work we may be known for our hard-driving energy, creative ideas, and competitive edge, attributes that would not always make for a well-functioning home life. Even worse, at work we may find ourselves driven by bottom-line thinking that leads us to treat others as commodities rather than as persons.

We can "shift" our manners, language, dress, and *even our values* to match the culture of a context. And yet this ease of adaptation can lead to inconsistency, even hypocrisy.

Notable examples of this "split" can be drawn from much-publicized corporate, government, and church scandals. We have too frequently heard stories of Christian leaders known for their commitment and wholehearted participation in their church communities who ran their organizations on a set of principles that emphasized personal greed rather than common good. Church leaders are not immune from this problem, as evidenced in those sad examples of corruption that become media fodder because of the radical split between personal behavior and public message. The existence of sin in our lives often leads to the presence of "secret identities." There is a side of our humanness that we believe is too distasteful or even too evil to be recognized. At times we fail to even acknowledge its presence to ourselves. More often we work hard to make sure that even those closest to us are unaware of its existence, kidding ourselves that it's "under control."

This slippage in values is not usually so dramatic and even occurs in those considered to be of exemplary character. In *Some Do Care: Contemporary Lives of Moral Commitment,* Jack Coleman, former president of Haverford College, describes an example from his own life of a time he felt his "integrity was less than complete."

> It was a situation of taking advantage of a potentially very generous donor . . . and this was the night, a night on which alcohol had flowed freely, when we were really going to push her and her husband hard on a commitment. . . . And late in the evening she made a commitment of a million dollars, and I — this is the point I'm embarrassed about — I told her, "you know, if you don't make a larger gift than that a very large amount of your money is going to go to the government. It's just going to go into welfare programs." And she went up to 4.5 million dollars. And I really am embarrassed about it. I knew this aspect of her character. I knew that she dreaded the idea of money going to welfare. And I don't like the fact that I used that. I was playing up to something in her which I didn't like and which is at odds with my own set of beliefs.[3]

Although most people will claim moral principles, these do not often predict moral behavior in everyday life.

While others might believe that the worthy ends of funding new programs justified the means, Coleman objected to his own behavior because he had "failed to treat the other person as you would want to be treated."[4]

Moral and Religious Identity

For many years psychologists in the field of moral development have sought to understand why people do or do not behave morally in real-life situations that demand moral decisions. Although most people will claim moral principles, these do not often predict moral behavior in everyday life. The concept of "moral identity" is providing a promising conceptual frame for understanding this human problem.

As an example, researchers have studied the lives of moral "exemplars": those individuals whose lives are marked by exceptional moral commitment. Although these individuals come from markedly diverse

3. A. Colby and W. Damon, *Some Do Care: Contemporary Lives of Moral Commitment* (New York: Free Press; New York: Maxwell Macmillan, 1992), 139.

4. Colby and Damon, *Some Do Care,* 139.

backgrounds and demonstrate their commitment in various ways, one of the personal traits they hold in common is a powerful congruence between their personal and their moral goals. Their integrity is such that they apply their religious and moral frameworks to every aspect of their lives. In other words, their moral identity is an ascendant framework that integrates and organizes their other "selves." For believers, one's religious identity is a broader concept within which moral identity is encased.

The Influence of Context

Leaders are responsible in significant ways for shaping the moral context of their organizations. "Leaders need to be concerned with the institutional value system which, after all, leads to the principles and standards that guide the practice of the people in the institution. Leaders owe a clear statement of the values of the organization."[5] This includes the values and standards that influence the behavior of all who work within its boundaries. It is precisely because men and women are able to respond almost automatically to the cues of their contexts, adapting their behavior to the norms of the situation, that leaders bear an enormous responsibility for setting the moral tone of their organizations.

One of the most famous of all psychology experiments, the Stanford Prison Experiment, illustrates this facet of human behavior. Following World War II, psychologists struggled to understand the question of what happens when you put good people in an evil place. For example, how could so many German citizens have participated without protest in the Holocaust? The Stanford study was designed to test the moral boundaries of the cream of American college students. The basement of one of the buildings on the Stanford campus was transformed into a mock prison. Student volunteers were randomly assigned to play the role of either prisoner or guard.

The experiment, which was designed to run for two weeks, had to be canceled after only six days due to the brutal behavior that began to be exhibited by the student-guards even late at night when the researchers weren't watching. The primary investigator, Phillip Zimbardo, describes what he found.

5. Max De Pree, *Leadership Is an Art* (New York: Doubleday, 1989), 14.

> We had created an overwhelmingly powerful situation — a situation in which prisoners were withdrawing and behaving in pathological ways, and in which some of the guards were behaving sadistically. Even the "good" guards felt helpless to intervene, and none of the guards quit while the study was in progress. Indeed, it should be noted that no guard ever came late for his shift, called in sick, left early, or demanded extra pay for overtime work. . . . Christina Maslach, a recent Stanford Ph.D. brought in to conduct interviews with the guards and prisoners, strongly objected when she saw our prisoners being marched on a toilet run, bags over their heads, legs chained together, hands on each other's shoulders. Filled with outrage, she said, "It's terrible what you are doing to these boys!" Out of fifty or more outsiders who had seen our prison, she was the only one who ever questioned its morality. Once she countered the power of the situation, however, it became clear that the study should be ended.[6]

Leaders should be concerned not only with the instrumental productivity and skill development of their workers but also with their personal well-being, including the welfare of their families.

While the Stanford experiment is an extreme example of a radical context (and hopefully none of us run our organizations like prisons!), it is a shocking example of the human characteristic for adaptation. Context can quickly overwhelm conscience.

Creating a Culture That Fosters an Integrated Christian Identity

One of the key dimensions of leadership is the importance of integrity. One definition of integrity is that the multiple identities of the leader are closely aligned and integrated under an ascendant values framework. The compassionate religious and moral values that provide personal

6. P. G. Zimbardo, "A Situationist Perspective on the Psychology of Evil: Understanding How Good People Are Turned into Perpetrators," in *The Social Psychology of Good and Evil*, ed. A. G. Miller (New York: Guilford Press, 2004).

meaning and purpose in the private sphere also are relevant and guide the foundational approach to leadership in the work culture. Leaders should be concerned not only with the instrumental productivity and skill development of their workers but also with their personal well-being, including the welfare of their families. Pastors should care not only about the size of their congregation but also about the condition of the neighborhood that surrounds the church. It should matter to captains of industry if their means of production cause environmental destruction. Stockholders should worry about the retirement plans of employees as much as they worry about annual profit margins.

As the promise of Christ is to unite a divided humanity under his rule, so too is Christ able to bring unity to our divided selves. Christ is the head of creation and all are subordinated to him. There is no area of culture or our daily lives that has not been affected by God's acts in Christ. Our identity in Christ should similarly rule over the "multiple selves" that populate our character. Our Christian self is not only relevant to our workplace, it is the priority. When our ultimate identity is anchored in the fact that we are God's creation, we have an answer to the question, "Who am I?" that has profound implications for our daily actions. We are given a place in creation, a purpose for our existence, and a set of values by which we can judge our decisions and actions for their "goodness." Despite our illusions of autonomy, as God's workmanship we are infinitely dependent on God.[7] Paul makes this point when he writes, *"In him we live and move and have our being"* (Acts 17:28).

What would it mean to claim and live with our Christian identity in ascendancy over each of our "selves"? How would our leadership be changed if gospel values took precedence over instrumental values? I would begin to address these questions with the added complication that even our Christian identity is multifaceted and significantly dependent upon the influence of others. Our Christian identity is built in dialogue with others who form the network of our close associates. We are embedded in relationships in which we are challenged, held accountable, and offered role models. For leaders, this often includes the reciprocal influence that comes from those who are otherwise considered followers.

7. Stanley J. Grenz, *Theology for the Community of God* (Nashville: Broadman and Holman, 1994), 131-32.

For Christian leaders a powerful influence is the quality of our relationship with God. In our relationship with God we are often in roles that appear to be at odds with our cultural conceptualizations and personal identity as leader. As Christians our identity is described in terms like "child of God," "follower of Christ," or "responsive servant." How can we integrate child, follower, and servant with our identity as leaders? Even more radically, can the values associated with these roles take precedence over the instrumental values that typically dominate the workplace?

Max De Pree illustrates this shift in thinking with a story from his own life. As he was sharing with his wife Esther his distress at laying off forty employees, she reminded him that his thinking was wrong. In fact, he should be thinking he was laying off forty families. As Max has written, "Since then I have never been able to think about individuals in the workplace without thinking of their families."[8]

Our identity in Christ should similarly rule over the "multiple selves" that populate our character.

Christian leaders are called to conduct their lives in ways that depart radically from the cultural definitions of leadership. Yet, too often, even those Christians who lead churches are culturally conditioned to implement methods and strategies at odds with Christ's rule. Too seldom is the health of an organization measured by the degree of compassion it has engendered; by the number of widows, orphans, and prisoners visited; or by the flourishing of the families whose lives are intertwined in its structures. And yet this is precisely the good work that God intended for us. "For we are his workmanship, created in Christ Jesus for good works, which God prepared beforehand, that we should walk in them" (Eph. 2:10 RSV).

8. Max De Pree, *Leadership Jazz* (New York: Currency Doubleday, 1992), 136.

11 Ministry Implications of Service

Nancy Ortberg

Editor's Introduction Servanthood in the pastorate seems to be about how we treat our congregants and perhaps how we treat our colleagues in ministry. But what does pastoral servanthood mean for people outside the church? In this chapter Nancy Ortberg, who heads up Axis ministry and has been a long-term mentee of Max De Pree, contends that servanthood is an important way that those who have become disgruntled with the church can be drawn back in.

A lot of things make up great leadership. Vision and strategy. Team building and motivation. Decision making and communication. The list could, and does, go on and on. So imagine the head-snap reaction when leaders read the words that give shape to the present volume: "The first responsibility of a leader is to define reality. The last is to say thank you. In between the two, the leader must become a servant and a debtor."

That's a *lot* of time as a servant. Not the typical perspective for leadership, but obviously a powerful one. And although the term "servant leadership" has been around for a while, the above quotation does a great deal to help us understand what that really means.

When I was on staff at Willow Creek Community Church, I had full days of leadership, which I loved. One day in particular, after a busy day of meetings and working on talks, I started down a long hall that led to the parking lot where my car was. Just before I got to the door, I ran into a couple with three small children. They appeared lost, and their English was about as good as my Spanish, so it took me a while to figure out that they were looking for the department at our church that handled food and housing issues.

At first glance it seemed to have been a while since they had access to much of either, and there was something that grew in my spirit as I helped them for about ten minutes, understanding their needs and walking them to the person who could meet those. I engaged in conversation as best I could, looking them in the eye, finding myself thinking about being kind in a way that might overcome the language barrier. I spoke to the children and showed them the toys put out for them to play with while their parents spoke to the church representative. And then I left them in the capable hands of another.

Now if you looked at a list of the things I did that day — led meetings, wrote a sermon, walked a family to the Community Care department — the first two would seem to qualify as the important stuff.

But here's the problem. I drove home that night with the very strong sense that, of everything I had done that day, those last ten minutes were the most important. That's not to say that the other stuff wasn't, but that they paled in comparison. As I tucked my kids into bed that night, I thought of those three kids, and sent up prayers of gratitude for the provisions of a roof and food for mine, and prayers of hope and direction for those things for that family.

The next day at work, that experience changed how I led meetings and prepared for a couple of talks coming up. My focus was different, my motivation clearer. I had seen some of the people that were the reason for the work I did, and it sharpened my direction. Servanthood will do that.

In Philippians 2 Paul tells us our attitude should be the same as Christ's. Okay, I can buy that. So what would that attitude be? Then Paul goes on to talk about servanthood. It is a passage so beautifully written it is referred to as the Christ Hymn. Most translations write (vv. 6, 7), "Who, although he was in very nature God . . . made himself nothing, taking the very nature of a servant." But Jerry Hawthorne, professor at Wheaton College, suggests that rather than concessive, it is causal: "Who because he was in very nature God . . . made himself nothing, taking the very nature of a servant."

When we serve, our hearts and our minds and our motivations and our actions are most closely linked with God's.

Not in spite of being God. But *because* he was God. Not in order to hide his "God-ness." But to reveal it. Hawthorne says God is most clearly seen in servanthood, because it is the nature of God to serve. So that when we serve, we become these accurate reflections of God to a world that isn't sure they know what he looks like. When we serve, our hearts and our minds and our motivations and our actions are most closely linked with God's. When we serve, we release the power of the nature of God into a world that is desperate for it. Our call to ministry is our call to serve.

Jimmy Long writes in his book *Generating Hope* about what new generations are looking for in the church and with God. He says there are now two conversions: the first is to community, the second is to God. These generations that largely grew up outside the church aren't necessarily ready to ask the God question yet, but are looking at God's people to see if they are living in ways that cause them to take note. If they are, those seekers may gravitate close enough to our community, and upon finding it to be rich and authentic, will eventually find the God that is in the center of that community.

These generations that largely grew up outside the church aren't necessarily ready to ask the God question yet, but are looking at God's people to see if they are living in ways that cause them to take note.

This has such huge implications for ministry in our church. Not to take away from our weekend programs, which often act as a way to build up believers as well as to attract seekers, but how we serve as the people of God becomes magnetic. How our church moves out into the neighborhoods and helps the underresourced and the AIDS patients, and visits those in prison and comes alongside the educational system, will become evidence of the authenticity of that.

When John and I lived in Chicago, we often invited one set of neighbors to church. Along with their polite "no thank you's" were those looks of "and please don't ask again." We knew them for about seven years before they came to church with us. They did not finally come because of our invitations. Nor because of their relationship with us, although that certainly made us the ones they came with. It was because someone they knew had been touched by the Cars Ministry at our church.

Every year a volunteer team of mechanics spruces up scores of donated cars and then gives them to single moms in the congregation. One of these moms was a teacher's aide who worked with our neighbors. She had been through a rough period in her life, and ended up with two kids to raise on a small salary. She had no car and no hope of getting one until the Cars Ministry.

Our neighbors came looking for us to ask if they could come to church with us.

"Uh, sure, yeah, okay!"

Servanthood is compelling. It is a magnetic force. Because it is the nature of God. Because people are made in his image.

So, are leadership and servanthood compatible? At first glance you might wonder. Much of what is written about leadership and much of what is lived out in the name of leadership lean toward the narcissistic, power-grabbing variety. Of course, in church work we would paint a veneer of spirituality over that to throw them off scent, and add the God trump card just so no one gets in our way. We've all seen it. Heck, we've all done it. But it leaves a bad taste in our mouths, hoping for a better way.

Here's where servanthood comes in. I found in the pages of De Pree's work on leadership such a beautiful dance between the strength of leadership, its vision, its hard declaration of reality, its momentum and implementation; and the kindness of leadership, its heart, its vision, its focus on the dignity of people and the nobility of service.

Leadership and servanthood are immensely compatible. Servanthood is the adjective for leadership. Servanthood is the focus and clarifying vision for leadership. Servanthood is the reason we lead. We need to rightly understand both words in order to live out their compatibility.

Servanthood is not weakness. Servanthood is not Mr. Rogers walking around making sure everyone is happy. It is not a mindless assent to compromise in order to keep the peace. It is not artificial harmony and people pleasing. Servanthood means to be of use to others, to assist them in ways that are for their good and their best. It is to provide for others, and that may be through services, goods, or direction. Servanthood helps. It moves alongside and makes the world better. Inherent in servanthood is the deep belief that people are of ultimate value and that serving them is a great thing.

Servanthood means to be of use to others, to assist them in ways that are for their good and their best.

I can make servanthood the adjective of nearly everything I do. I can have the mind of a servant when I prepare a message, lead a meeting, return a phone call, roast a chicken, or pick up the dry cleaning. How I treat people, how I move the focus from me to them, how I thank them — all have the potential to allow me to serve. When I am in the process of hiring someone, I almost always take the person out to a meal and watch how he or she treats the waitstaff. Servanthood matters.

But just as servanthood matters, leadership means something. It is not a nothing word, simply there to give servanthood something to describe. Leadership is a call to action, to purposefully move people and organizations in a direction of a preferred future. Leadership has energy and passion and is concerned with movement and alignment and growth and development. And while all those things involve enthusiasm, they also involve pain, and they involve the possibility of hidden agendas. Perhaps these are the touch points where leadership and servanthood seem at odds with each other. But it does not have to be so. Let's look at what it would mean to be a servant leader in areas of ministry leadership.

When I am in the process of hiring someone, I almost always take the person out to a meal and watch how he or she treats the waitstaff.

As a final thought to propel us toward that, let's revisit the final phrase of the quote with which we began this reflection: "The first responsibility of a leader is to define reality. The last is to say thank you. In between the two, the leader must become a servant and a debtor."

A *debtor.*

That is shockingly counterintuitive. Most leaders think in terms of what others owe them. Loyalty, energy, work ethic — another endless list.

De Pree challenges the leader to think in terms of what he/she owes others. That kind of thinking has the potential to shape the leader into a servant. A servant who leads.

Preaching. What are the questions I am asking as I prepare my messages? Do they revolve around how I am doing, how this will come across, whether people who hear it will think I am smart, witty, and wise? Or do the predominate questions I am asking as I research and think and write revolve around the people in my congregation who will hear the message?

I can serve when I preach, primarily if I am living in the tension of what the people need and who God is. Many pastors who work on their messages only behind closed doors miss the former. They do not know their people well enough to know what they are struggling with and wondering about their jobs, their families, and their lives. Preaching is not an isolated activity. It serves when it is integrated in relationships.

I do leadership development for organizations and from time to time find myself in a coaching role with leaders. Not long ago I had a conversation with a pastor and asked him how well he knew the daily struggles, fears, and joys of his congregants.

"Not well at all," was his reply.

We talked through ways in which he might get to know those better and add that to the great preparation he was already doing for his sermons. It wasn't long before the joy and effectiveness of his preaching increased. It was already good, but it got better and took on the posture of a servant, a debtor.

What he owed his congregation was knowing them.

Meetings. Much of the work of leadership happens in meetings. In fact, I think one of the diagnostic tools for detecting leadership qualities is to ask a person if he or she would rather work on a message or go to a meeting. Most teachers would rather be shot in the head than go to a meeting. Leaders are weird that way — they'd rather attend the meeting.

Meetings are the place where vision is shaped and strategy is born. They are where organizational culture is lived out and where decisions are made and personal and professional development takes place.

Here the work of a leader becomes to shape the questions we are asking and answering at our meetings to how we serve our constituency. Part of the answer will be in their felt needs, part of it will be the leader's decisions about where the people and the organization need to move.

Organizational questions at a meeting that serve are: What ministries do we need to effectively assist people in knowing God and becoming more like Christ? How do we lead those ministries in such a way that they grow in their effectiveness and their vibrancy? Which ministries are not effectively doing that, and when should we stop those? How do we evaluate the answers to both of those questions?

Mediocre ministries do not serve. Ineffective and unfocused churches are not simply led poorly, they are serving poorly. The power of the church is in its servanthood; the relentless question of a leader becomes, "How are we doing at that?"

Personal questions at a meeting that serve are: Where is each person in this circle at in his or her development as a leader and as a follower of

Christ, and how can I help facilitate and shape that person's movement to the next level?

I believe strongly that leadership is the promise of development. Great leaders serve the immediate people they lead by both knowing them and growing them. Leaders need opportunities, challenges, and relationship to grow, and my constant question becomes "what?" in each of those areas.

For five of the eight years that I worked at Willow Creek, I led a ministry called Axis. Axis was the postmodern ministry designed to reach the "eighteen-to-twenty-something generation." We had two weekend services in the gym (Saturday evenings and late Sunday mornings) while "big church" met in the main auditorium. It was with the Axis staff and larger community that I learned some of my deepest lessons about serving as ministry, and serving as leadership.

When I first arrived, as is often the case in times of transition, the staff met me with distance and suspicion. They had been through a lot of difficulty in the preceding year, some of which I knew about, most of which I probably didn't. They were scarred and cynical, and they did not want me there. Not much of this was hidden.

To serve, to lead, I had to give them time. A number of mentors suggested that I move to fire those I wasn't sure about within the first six weeks. Wait any longer, they warned, and it will be too late and communicate your own lack of courage.

I think there are times when that is probably spot-on advice. I sensed this wasn't one of them. I sensed that to lead well, I needed to show up every day and build trust. Building trust does not mean spending endless hours having coffee and talking, or falling in a blindfolded heap into each other's arms. Trust is born of competency and character and vulnerability.

So we had meetings to plan weekend services, and to design our small-group structure, and to develop our serving teams to help the underresourced. In those meetings we made decisions based on vision, we saw progress, and I admitted I didn't know all I needed to know to lead this ministry and would need to learn from them. I had some difficult conversations.

One guy in particular continued in his deep cynicism for months. Six, to be exact. I remember it was six months because it was at that point that I invited him to my office. Sometimes trust building happens in difficult conversations. I told him I thought that cynicism was a lack of courage. And we spent the next hour talking about that concept. I added to it the concept that I was not going to go away, and therefore he probably had some decisions to make.

The next day he wrote "Cynicism is a lack of courage" on an 8-inch by 12-inch poster board and taped it inside his office, above the door, so that every time he left his office he was reminded. He and I had one of the best working relationships in my time at Axis.

And there was reciprocity. It wasn't just me leading him, although that's the way the job descriptions described it. Part of servant leadership is the humility to learn from all directions. There were numerous times that his direct conversation with me caused me to either change my mind or dig a little deeper into my soul to connect with more Christlike motivations for leading.

I served as a leader in the Axis ministry by having direct and repeated connections with our key leaders. I met with them on a regular basis, and not only trained and discipled them, but also knew them. Really knew them, liked them, loved them. And they, me. So that when I prepared a message, or thought through a series, or planned a meeting, I had them in mind. I knew their work world, their relational world, their doubts and fears, their joys and stories. I had their permission to lead because of it.

Part of servant leadership is the humility to learn from all directions.

I did not do any of this perfectly. I didn't even do it well all the time. But I did it. I did it often and with great gratitude. Servanthood lives between the acceptance of what is and the hope of what can be. It is the dominion of God.

TASK 3 Saying Thanks

12 The Challenge of Gratitude

Richard J. Mouw

Editor's Introduction In many ways gratitude seems only tangentially related to the serious business of leadership. In the pastorate gratitude can be construed as an occasional activity embedded in the local routines of the church year. Gratitude has to do with presenting flowers on Secretary's Day and hosting a Thank You Dinner after a successful stewardship campaign. In this essay Richard Mouw, president of Fuller Theological Seminary, asserts that leadership needs to be continually grounded in gratitude if it is to avoid serious distortion. Leadership, for Christians, is ultimately about gratitude. We must be grateful both to God and to our followers, who in many ways give us our roles as leaders. Things go wrong when our leadership begins to feel expected or autonomous. The practice of saying thank you reminds us that it is not.

What do those of us who lead owe to our followers? I think most of us, if asked this question, would start talking about honesty, integrity, wisdom, accountability — those strike me as the obvious kinds of answers. I must confess that gratitude does not come quickly to my mind as something that belongs on the list. I have often made reference, in writings and speeches, to the familiar line that "the first responsibility of a leader is to define reality." But I must confess that I have not spent much time thinking about the sentence that immediately follows it, that a leader's last responsibility "is to say thank you." I will try to remedy my past neglect here by reflecting on the role of gratitude in the life of a leader.

One reason why the statement about defining reality is easy to talk about is that it reminds most people of an obvious truth. Leaders need to know what they are doing. They need to take account of all relevant facts. And their fact gathering should be integrated with creative thinking about an organization's past, present, and future, resulting in what is called these days "vision-casting." All of that seems quite obvious when we think about it. And yet leaders need constantly to be reminded of it, obvious as it may be, given the constant temptation to attend only to the immediate practical details of organizational life.

That leaders have a responsibility to say thank you, on the other hand, is not quite so obvious. Of course, we all know that we — simply as human beings — must regularly express our gratitude to God, on whom we are dependent for the very air we breathe. And most of us would acknowledge the pragmatic utility of saying thank you to our followers: a "one-minute manager" approach, for example, might suggest that if leaders want to be seen as effective in their role, it is a good idea regularly to tell folks how much you appreciate what they are doing for the organization, etc. But that kind of saying-thank-you is not the only way to understand this concept.

That leaders have a responsibility to say thank you is not so obvious.

The fact is, whether saying thank you actually "works" is up for grabs. If a leader merely wants to get his or her way, intimidation might be a more effective strategy than saying thank you. We need to consider the possibility that gratitude is not just a potentially useful means to a pragmatically chosen end but a question of the basic character of a leader. To be a good leader — the kind of person who *deserves* to be called a leader — one must express gratitude.

But how does the business of saying thank you manifest itself in a leader's life? The temporal language De Pree uses in ranking the two responsibilities he highlights — defining reality is "first," saying thank you is "last" — certainly can be taken in a straightforward chronological sense. On such an interpretation, the advice would go something like this: *at the beginning of your leadership emphasize the defining of reality, but before it is over remember also to say thank you.* And this is certainly good counsel. Defining reality is an ongoing process in leadership: no decision or initiative should be pursued without it. Saying thank you, however, can be seen as more "episodic." There are *occasions* to express gratitude, and they certainly arise when one comes to the conclusion of one's service as a leader. And for a Christian, there is also *the* end: that ultimate Final Accounting when we each will acknowledge from the depths of our being that everything — including the opportunities to exercise leadership — has been a gift of grace for which humble gratitude to the divine Giver is the only appropriate response.

But there is also a nonchronological sense of the notion of the "last" responsibility of a leader. It is the sense of "final" that is at work in the phrase "in the final analysis." Thus, while the primary thing a leader must attend to is the defining of reality, it is also important to recognize that *in the final analysis* leadership is about gratitude. This is the meaning that Walter Wright is getting at earlier in this volume when he says that the saying-thank-you responsibility in Max De Pree's thought is connected to a necessary sense of *dependence.*

While the primary thing a leader must attend to is the defining of reality, it is also important to recognize that in the final analysis leadership is about gratitude.

I once heard Warren Bennis tell a story about being president of the University of Cincinnati. He had been in that office for about six years when one day at a faculty meeting a person asked him whether he loved his work. He was thrown by the question and stumbled through a few comments that did not really answer the question directly. As he drove home that day, Bennis reported, he had a deep sense of failure. He came to realize that if he could not give a straightforward positive answer to the question whether he loved being the leader of that university, he had no right to continue in the role. Leaders, he said, owe it to their followers to assure them that they love being in their role.

I thought a lot about Bennis's story, an exercise that inspired me to reflect much on my own attitude toward leadership. Do I love being president of Fuller Seminary? I finally came to a point where I could honestly say yes to that question. And not long afterward I told the faculty that I loved being their leader.

That answer, while genuine, does not come easily to me. I am tempted to hold back from giving my all to being an administrative leader of a theological school. Part of me still loves to do the things that occupied my professional life long before I became a president: teaching, scholarship, and "public intellectual" kinds of activities. None of those, of course, are bad things — nor is a continuing involvement in them incompatible with my leadership obligations. But the spiritual temptation for me is to hang on to them as separate *identities,* to reassure myself that if I fail in my presidency I will have something to fall back on. To the degree that I am hedging my bets in this way, I am not being a responsible leader.

Again, the issue is not the sorts of things I want to *do* as a president, but rather the *spirit* of my doing. To use Walter Wright's term, I must regularly cultivate a spirit of *dependence.* And that spirit of dependence is closely linked to a habitual inner state of gratitude.

In our larger culture leaders are often very ungrateful people. Much of this emanates from the way leaders come to see themselves. In one of his studies of role theory the sociologist Erving Goffman tells of a young man who participated in an on-campus reserved-officer program as a university student, and upon graduation entered the military full time as a commissioned officer. During his first days in his new career, walking the military base in full uniform, the young man felt like he was at a costume party. And each time a person of lower rank saluted him, he was taken by surprise.

A year later the man is on leave in a resort, wearing civilian clothes. Walking down a street, he is approached by enlisted persons in uniform, and he is momentarily offended when they do not salute him. But then he remembers that because he is not in uniform, they have no way of knowing about his rank. In the course of a year, Goffman explains, the young man has internalized his role. His rank now "fits" him perfectly and he has come to expect, instinctively, the behaviors due to him because of his status.

All of us in leadership positions need to monitor that tendency toward internalization. I have met some pastors whose manner of ordinary conversation sounds a lot like old-fashioned pulpit oration. Sometimes I wonder whether they roll over in bed in the morning and greet their spouses with a formal liturgical salutation!

I have come to expect to be treated in certain ways because of my "rank." There are dangers that lurk here for the leader.

But let me pick on myself instead. During one of my first days as an administrator I was working in my office during the noon hour. My assistant came in and asked me what she could bring me for lunch. I was taken aback, and replied that she did not "need to bother." Her response: "It is not a bother; this is my job." Many years later my instincts have changed. I no longer feel awkward when an assistant offers to do something for me. I have come to expect to be treated in certain ways because of my "rank." There are dangers that lurk here for the leader. I need constantly to remind myself of what it was like at the beginning — especially of the gratitude that I felt when people offered to come to my assistance, even though they could accurately say, "This is my job."

This sense of gratitude is even more appropriate when dealing with a volunteer force. I need to express special gratitude regularly to seminary trustees, who work hard for the cause of theological education without any remuneration. (Indeed, they contribute much to the fund from which others receive remuneration!) And pastors are even more dependent on volunteer labor than seminary administrators.

Leaders rely on the commitments of others, an obvious cause for gratitude. But the need to be grateful goes even deeper. In his classic study of leadership, James MacGregor Burns observes that "transforming leadership" — which is far superior to "transactional leadership" in his accounting — "raises the level of human conduct and ethical aspiration of both leader and led, and thus it has a transforming effect on both."[1] His point here is profound. When healthy leadership occurs, it brings positive changes to the person of the leader. Leaders, like their followers, are brought to new levels of both "human conduct" and "ethical aspiration." Our gratitude toward our followers, then, has to do with the ways they have transformed us in a manner that would not have happened without our participation in the leader-follower relationship.

Leaders rely on the commitments of others, an obvious cause for gratitude.

All this takes on a special texture when seen in a Christian perspective. The Bible makes it clear: we need all the help we can get simply as human beings, to say nothing of as leaders.

> All we like sheep have gone astray;
> we have all turned to our own way.
>
> (Isa. 53:6)[2]

1. James MacGregor Burns, *Leadership* (New York: Harper and Row, 1978), 20.
2. All Bible references here are from the New Revised Standard Version.

In an important sense, leadership is a key theme in the Bible. Having created human beings, God immediately commands them to "have dominion" in the garden where he has placed them (Gen. 1:26). And in the very last chapter of the Bible, at the very end of the marvelous vision of the new creation, the apostle notes that redeemed humanity "will reign forever and ever" (Rev. 22:5). These two positive portrayals of human leadership, however, bracket a long and tragic story about leadership. The first human pair are not content to care for the creation under the sovereign rule of God. They give in to the Tempter's false promise that they themselves "will be like God," defining reality in terms of their own attempts at "knowing good and evil" (Gen. 3:5).

Much of the biblical story after that, then, focuses on the patterns and results of fallen leadership. For example, when the elders of Israel request of the prophet Samuel that they be given a human "king to govern us, like other nations" (1 Sam. 8:4-6), the Lord tells Samuel to inform them of the oppressive ways of human leaders under fallen conditions (8:8-18). And even though later on, in his farewell address to the people, Samuel outlines the conditions whereby it can still "be well" with the nation and their human king, the subsequent history of leadership in the Old Testament is a disappointing one.

But it was in the midst of constant disillusionment with the ways of their leaders that the people of God were given a message from the inspired prophets, that the Lord would someday provide a leader who would never disappoint them — one who would carry divine authority "on his shoulders," and who would be given the very name "Wonderful Counselor" (Isa. 9:6). This leader would be a gentle nurturer, who, while he "comes with might," nonetheless

> will feed his flock like a shepherd;
>   he will gather the lambs in his arms,
> and carry them in his bosom,
>   and gently lead the mother sheep.
>
> (Isa. 40:11)

It is this ancient promise that Christians believe was fulfilled in Jesus of Nazareth, who, when "he saw a great crowd . . . had compassion for them, because they were like sheep without a shepherd; and he began to teach them many things" (Mark 6:34).

A key teaching that we have learned from Jesus is the very idea of servant leadership. It is in connection with this pattern of leading that saying thank you comes into the picture in a very special way. As people who need all the help we can get, it is gratifying to be offered both a model and the requisite strength to be a leader who is in turn led by Jesus. But once we actually get into that relationship with the true Servant-leader, we realize that by being his follower we receive in great measure the things that James MacGregor Burns says we should expect also from our relationships with our followers: in Christ, in a very special way, we are brought to new levels of both "human conduct" and "ethical aspiration" — important features of the abundant life that is promised to all who walk the path of discipleship.

We can hope to counteract the widespread influence of the spirit of entitlement only by a "schooling" in our own congregations that encourages the cultivation of the virtue of gratitude.

Social commentators often observe these days that we are living in a culture that is increasingly characterized by a pervasive sense of "entitlement," by which they mean that people make a lot of demands, and they do so with a clear sense that they *deserve* what they are asking for. Another way of putting this is that our culture is becoming increasingly characterized by ingratitude. The church must address this syndrome, and in a way that goes far beyond merely preaching an annual sermon on the subject when Thanksgiving Day rolls around.

The Lutheran theologian Ronald Thiemann has observed that local congregations should function as "'schools of public virtue,' communities that seek to form the kind of character necessary for public life."[3] We can hope to counteract the widespread influence of the spirit of entitlement only by a "schooling" in our own congregations that encourages the cultivation of the virtue of gratitude. And as Christian leaders we can make some good progress in this by being the kind of people who demonstrate on a regular basis that we see it as very important to say thank you.

3. Ronald Thiemann, *Constructing Public Theology: The Church in a Pluralistic Culture* (Louisville: Westminster John Knox, 1991), 43.

13 Gratitude as Access to Meaning

Mark Lau Branson

Editor's Introduction Of course, gratitude is the right attitude for pastors to cultivate, but is it also connected to perception? Do grateful leaders see reality more accurately than those who are not grateful? In this essay Mark Lau Branson, who teaches practical theology at Fuller Theological Seminary, demonstrates how gratitude is fundamentally related to our epistemology. By focusing on our gratitude for what is working in the church rather than trying to tackle problems, we allow the church to be shaped by the unfolding story of God's faithfulness among the people of God in a local setting.

Gratitude and wisdom are intertwined. If a leadership team is to lead with insight and wisdom, it must have the capacities and skills to discern the specificities of God's grace among a people, in the midst of activities, given a certain context. Gratefulness is a characteristic that can be developed through practices — habits of attentiveness, prayer, conversation, query, and numerous aspects of relationships and management. Gratefulness is not just a personality trait, it is a way of knowing, and it is a choice. Henri Nouwen writes, "Gratitude as a discipline involves a conscious choice. I can choose to be grateful even when my emotions and feelings are still steeped in hurt and resentment. It is amazing how many occasions present themselves in which I can choose gratitude instead of a complaint. . . . The choice for gratitude rarely comes without some real ef-

Gratefulness is not just a personality trait, it is a way of knowing, and it is a choice.

fort. But each time I make it, the next choice is a little easier, a little freer, a little less self-conscious."[1]

As leaders, we work in the midst of circumstances that might make wisdom. The relationship between gratefulness and knowing — between an expectant and appreciative stance to the work of leadership and the information that is available for wisdom — is the focus of this chapter. Leaders need information; we find and create knowledge in our interaction with collaborators and context.

Interpretive Leadership

Leadership teams have responsibilities that include interpretive, relational, and implemental spheres. Interpretive leadership — our work with meanings — is generative only if linked wisely with our relational leadership and implemental leadership.[2] A finance committee may be able to sustain its work in simply performing tasks ("implementation"), but leaders in the organization, and hopefully on the finance committee, live into the generative *meanings* of stewardship, generosity, and the social cohesion created by sharing resources. (This is at the root of the meaning of *koinonia,* often translated as fellowship.) Gratitude is important in all three spheres of leadership; the focus here is on interpretive matters.

When a leadership team works together and interacts with their organization, they assume certain meanings, they learn about meanings that members carry, they sanction meanings, they shape meanings. Interpretive leadership creates an environment and provides opportunities and resources for the organization (which is a "community of interpreters") as participants converse about God, texts, context, and the congregation. Organizations too easily pass on structures and functions while leaving behind narratives and meanings; interpretive leadership creates a more meaningful and holistic common life. The fruit of interpretive leadership is in the truthfulness, adequacy, ownership, and embodiment

1. Henri Nouwen, *The Return of the Prodigal* (New York: Doubleday, 1992), 85.

2. For more on this leadership triad, see Mark Lau Branson, "Forming God's People," in *Leadership in Congregations,* ed. Richard Bass (Herndon, Va.: Alban Institute, 2007), 97-107; and "Ecclesiology and Leadership for the Missional Church," in *The Missional Church in Context: Helping Congregations Develop Contextual Ministry,* ed. Craig Van Gelder (Grand Rapids: Eerdmans, 2007), 94-125.

of meanings. So any discussion about "youth ministry" or "pastoral leadership" or "housing" will require more than some functional or procedural decisions — participants need to enter into interpreting past, current, and future narratives and imaginaries.[3]

Interpretive leaders need to gain insights into how meanings have been shaped in the church. They look for connections between biblical and traditional meanings as the church has embodied them. What did it mean to baptize children or youth? What did it mean to raise children in faith? What was the role of the family in faith development? How do festivals and holidays shape faithful families? What is the role of staff in relationship to youth and their families? Also, since other societal forces have plans for children, how did this church endorse or counter the society's agenda? For example, since the society needs a "mobile workforce" (that readily leaves geographic roots) and new generations of consumers (who can be shaped by the marketing industry), in what ways has the church cooperated with or countered that agenda? How have previous generations of the church's adults embodied Christian faith — which is to ask, what models are available? (A similar set of queries can be made about worship, or mission, or leadership.)

If interpretive leaders have the work of creating environments for conversations — which is a primary work of leaders — what must they do to have a generative conversation about current challenges, like those in youth ministry or appropriate engagement with culture? Often strategic planning is used to identify and analyze problems, then solutions are proposed and implemented. While strategic planning can at times be helpful in limited arenas, to engage some aspects of technical work, it can easily avoid the most important conversations and too quickly jump to solutions.[4] Strategic planning at times gives participants the impres-

3. Social imaginaries (how a group of people imagine themselves; how they see their own lives and futures) shape the behaviors and thinking of groups. The imaginaries are shaped *by* numerous forces — cultures, families, economics and marketing, politics, and peers. Leaders make little difference if they cannot work with the social imagination of a group. See Charles Taylor, *Modern Social Imaginaries* (Durham, N.C.: Duke University Press, 2004).

4. Ronald Heifetz addresses the limits of strategic planning in his comparisons of "adaptive leadership" and "technical leadership" in *Leadership without Easy Answers* (Cambridge: Harvard University Press, 1994). See also Ronald Heifetz and Marty Linsky, *Leadership on the Line* (Boston: Harvard Business School, 2002).

sion that they are in control — which is often misleading. Churches have narrative resources in ancient texts and in their own experiences that can reshape conversations toward more complex changes. Theological assumptions underlie this mode of interpretive leadership — that God has provided what is needed for a church to walk in faithfulness.[5] We access those resources through a stance of grateful awareness. Without a foundational awareness of and embodiment of grace, leaders will not know what they need to know.

Appreciative Inquiry

A West Coast urban church had been through numerous changes — the arrival of a new pastor, many elderly members "crossing over Jordan," and the stresses created by a consultant who created divisiveness. Pastor Jean Burch gathered the members around tables for a conversation. "In all of your time at our church, when have you been most energized, most inspired? Who was involved? What was your role?" Soon the room was filled with animated conversations. With this and other questions, Pastor Burch led participants into memories that generated new cohesion and courage. This was more than "don't worry, be happy" — the content of the stories provided insights and wisdom that significantly changed the church's reality. There were apologies that brought reconciliation; some relatively new participants became seriously engaged. One board member said, "Before today, it was like we were married but we'd forgotten why. Now we remember why we are married. It almost feels like we've fallen in love again."

In Appreciative Inquiry, leaders have chosen to give unique attention to the most positive and generative resources in an organization.

This church embraced a model of organizational development that pays unique attention to positive narratives and fosters leaders who become more competent at identifying generative assets. This process is

5. Alan Roxburgh and Fred Romanuk address fundamental theological and leadership matters in *The Missional Leader* (San Francisco: Jossey-Bass, 2006).

called Appreciative Inquiry (AI).[6] This mode of shaping conversations is rooted in "action research" in which leaders intentionally enter into an organization's conversations through research and questions. Research is not passive — any inquiry will shape an organization's conversations and practices. Some methods of query can actually *limit* wisdom and options even as facts are surfaced. This happens because organizations are shaped by their conversations, including the conversations we create through questions or the communication we shape through reports and mission statements and plans. In Appreciative Inquiry, leaders have chosen to give unique attention to the most positive and generative resources in an organization.

Any organization that gives most of its attention to problems will be shaped more by the problems than by the life-giving narratives and resources that are present in their midst.

A typical approach to management and organizational change focuses on problems that need to be solved. Sometimes this is a specific sequence: name the problem, search for the causes, propose and analyze possible solutions, implement a plan, then start the cycle again. While there are legitimate times for a problem-solving approach, any organization that gives most of its attention to problems will be shaped more by the problems than by the life-giving narratives and resources that are present in their midst. In the earlier example, if a church keeps trying new proposals to solve the problem of a dearth of youth, they are not likely to live into their most generative opportunities. Similarly, church research that continually gives time to mismatched demographics or reshuffling a declining savings account will give all its energy to the least helpful conversations. Language theory helps us understand that what we talk about becomes our reality.[7] So if our

6. For a more thorough treatment of Appreciative Inquiry for churches, see Mark Lau Branson, *Memories, Hopes, and Conversations: Appreciative Inquiry and Congregational Change* (Herndon, Va.: Alban Institute, 2004); for an excellent general text on AI, see Diana Whitney and Amanda Trosten-Bloom, *The Power of Appreciative Inquiry* (San Francisco: Berrett-Koehler, 2003).

7. Social construction theory teaches that we live in and understand our reality mainly through language. We perceive and sort and act in our world in ways that are dependent on and shaped by vocabulary and grammar. We thus generate meanings and futures together. See Vivian Burr, *An Introduction to Social Constructionism* (London: Routledge, 1995).

questions and research and meetings and parking lot conversations are all about problems, we will perpetually live in a reality that is primarily a problem. There may be other very important resources available — assets, hopes, positive experiences, generative imagination — but if our conversations operate only in the "problem mode," we cut ourselves off from wisdom and warp reality around a spiral of negation.[8]

Several basic assumptions are important to Appreciative Inquiry. These are based in various fields of organizational and communication theory:[9]

- In every organization, there are positive narratives and important resources.
- What we focus on becomes our reality.
- Asking questions influences the group.
- People have more confidence in the journey to the future when they carry forward parts of the past.
- If we carry parts of the past into the future, they should be what is best about the past.
- The language we use creates our reality.
- Organizations are heliotropic; like plants seeking the sun, they bend toward energy.

These assumptions form the basis for leaders to enter into various groups with questions that will surface the organization's most important narratives.

While Appreciative Inquiry is implemented in several ways in an organization, five basic processes are always important.[10] (1) Choose the

8. Many church-planning tools use what is called "gap theory": your church has certain lacks, an expert or "successful" church has the answers, so leaders just need to work their church across the gap. An alternative framework that is consistent with Appreciative Inquiry is "diffusion of innovation." See especially Patrick Keifert, *We Are Here Now: A New Missional Era* (Eagle, Idaho: Allelon, 2006).

9. I have adapted materials from Sue Annis Hammond, *The Thin Book of Appreciative Inquiry,* 2nd ed. (Plano, Tex.: Thin Book Publishing Co., 1998), 24; Suresh Srivastva and David Cooperrider, eds., *Appreciative Management and Leadership,* rev. ed. (Euclid, Ohio: Williams Custom Publishing, 1999), 117; and Dennis Campbell, *Congregations as Learning Communities* (Bethesda, Md.: Alban Institute, 2000).

10. Jane Magruder Watkins and Bernard Mohr, *Appreciative Inquiry: Change at the Speed of Imagination* (San Francisco: Jossey-Bass/Pfeiffer, 2001), 39.

positive as the focus of inquiry. (2) Inquire into the stories of life-giving forces. (3) Locate themes that appear in the stories and select topics for further inquiry. (4) Create shared images for a preferred future. (5) Find innovative ways to create that future. Sometimes these processes are sequenced through four steps such as initiate, inquire, imagine, innovate. It is important that an organization create a process through all these steps — otherwise the insights and wisdom are lost.[11] Here is how AI compares with the common problem-solving approaches:[12]

Problem Solving

"Felt Need"
Identification of Problem

↓

Analysis of Causes

↓

Analysis of Possible Solutions

↓

Action Plan/Treatment

Appreciative Inquiry

Initiate AI by introducing leaders to theory and practice, deciding focus, and developing initial steps to discover the organization's "best."

↓

Inquire concerning "the best" of the organization's narratives, practices, and imaginations.

↓

Imagine "what might be" by interpreting the interviews, taking the risk of imagination, and building toward consensus concerning "what should be."

↓

Innovate "what will be" through discourse, commitment, equipping, and experiments.

If church leaders want to increase their access to positive narratives and resources, and bring other church participants into creative visioning,

11. The continual process of interpretation, when linked with relationships and implementation, includes conversations, discernment, and imagination in relationship with innovation, experiments, commitments, and evaluations. This ongoing rhythm between study/reflection and engagement/action is embedded in the word "praxis"; see Branson, "Ecclesiology and Leadership for the Missional Church." Discernment as a congregational practice is served well by Danny Morris and Charles Olsen, *Discerning God's Will Together* (Bethesda, Md.: Alban Institute, 1997).

12. I have adapted this from Watkins and Mohr, *Appreciative Inquiry,* 14, and Hammond, *Thin Book,* 24.

they should shape questions to foster generative conversations. These are samples of general questions and some that are specific to some aspect of church life:

- In all your years at our church, when have you been most engaged, most energized? Who was involved? What happened? What was your role?
- Think of a time when you thought some leaders at our church were especially helpful and you had a sense of clarity, hopefulness, and belonging. The leaders may have been staff persons or volunteers. Tell me about your most positive experiences of leadership in our church.
- Concerning our relationships with each other, what characterizes us at our best? How would you describe those times when you have seen Christian behaviors and qualities that have increased the congregation's social health, faithfulness, and unity?
- In all the ways we connect with the local community, the nation, and the world, what do you believe are the most important and meaningful elements of our church's outreach? Describe those times when you believe the church was most faithful or effective in missional activities.
- If you had three wishes about the relationships among youth and adults in our church, what would those wishes be?[13]

When a church has conversations around these kinds of questions, the leaders are reshaping reality. The conversations themselves change the people, and thereby change the future. Instead of creating and nurturing a problem-centered corporate life, AI questions foster generative relationships and imaginaries. For example, while the church might have been discussing an age-segmented, program-centered approach to youth, they may learn from Scripture and their own stories that intergenerational activities and conversations are worth new attention. Through such practices of appreciation, leaders gain access to stories — and to the winds of the Holy Spirit — and critical knowledge is increased.

13. It is important to use language about "wishes." If the questions use "should" or "ought" language, inappropriate expectations are easily formed. The AI process is about the circular shaping of language and church participants to foster a highly participative creative movement into new imaginaries.

The AI process can work on overall church life or on some specific area — like outreach, leadership, or discipleship. The queries lead to conversations that foster imagination, innovation, and new experiments. When another West Coast church completed a fairly large process, they decided to focus on the life of their older members. Because the first process created new energy and conversations, a new set of questions was created and a team carried the process from interviews through the development of generative themes to new "provocative proposals" that led to experiments. These proposals are based in the stories and the hopes of interviewees, and they are crafted to describe a new reality that is a few years in the future. There were three new provocative proposals. Here is one:

> We are a congregation blessed by Nisei (second-generation Japanese Americans; the youngest in their seventies) — a generation that has gained wisdom and grace through years of service and friendships. We have been inspired to move beyond our Japanese hesitancy and have learned that it is honorable not only to serve others and to give gifts but also to understand our own needs and to work together to form an interdependent congregation. We are continually encouraged and equipped by our pastoral staff and other skilled professionals to assess our needs and resources. We are inspired to reach beyond our congregation into our circles of friendships and the neighborhood around us, believing God is the author of our relationships. First Presbyterian Church, Altadena, is rooted in networks of holistic care, and the Nisei lead our intergenerational congregation in these joyful and innovative ways of meeting day-to-day needs such as health care, house maintenance, transportation, money management, shopping, and nutrition. We are grateful that in our daily words and work, in giving and receiving, God enlarges our lives and forms us as a caring and generous people.

These conversations and proposals have led to numerous experiments and innovative activities. Because these new activities came out of the members themselves, there is no sense that these are imported programs; the members themselves paid attention to stories and imaginations, and led the way to new ways of being church.

The apostle Paul taught the value of paying attention to generative narratives: "Finally, beloved, whatever is true, whatever is honorable, whatever is just, whatever is pure, whatever is pleasing, whatever is commendable, if there is any excellence and if there is anything worthy of praise, think about these things" (Phil. 4:8 NRSV).

Paul on Gratitude

Wisdom is born of gratefulness; understanding comes from being embedded in the ancient stories and in the recent winds of the Spirit. God's initiatives have always been toward creating and sustaining social entities (Israel, churches) that are fully engaged in God's love for them and for the world. Scriptures provide us with numerous stories about the life-giving presence and work of God — always noting the difference between grateful receptivity, trust, and participation ("faith") and dismissive denial and nonparticipation ("sin"). Without a fundamental orientation of gratitude — being grateful to God and appreciative of God's initiatives — leaders cannot see what they must see. The psalmists and prophets are always basing their work — their leadership of the people — in the narratives of God's gracious initiatives. Contemporary leaders need to create conversations that attend to the ways God has been present and active — in the decades of the church's life and in the current realities. The apostle Paul models this approach to leadership and nurtures it among others.

The psalmists and prophets are always basing their work — their leadership of the people — in the narratives of God's gracious initiatives.

The churches Paul founded and sought to influence were organizations of grace and sin, faithfulness and flaws. Even though each letter addressed internal and external threats, they all began with thanksgiving and affirmation.[14] Here Paul and his team addressed the Thessalonians: "We always give thanks to God for all of you and mention you in our prayers, constantly remembering before our God and Father your work of faith and labor of love and steadfastness of hope in our Lord Jesus Christ. . . . And you

14. Even in the letter to the Galatians, which omits the traditional epistolary opening of thanksgiving, Paul still notes that it was their responsiveness to God's grace that set the church's foundations.

became imitators of us and of the Lord, for in spite of persecution you received the word with joy inspired by the Holy Spirit, so that you became an example to all the believers in Macedonia and in Achaia . . . in every place your faith in God has become known" (1 Thess. 1:2-3, 6-8b NRSV).

The leaders of the Thessalonian church were facing contextual challenges (persecution along with various societal seductions) and internal traits that undermined faithfulness (conflicts, apathy, fear, vengeance). Paul could have recommended that they hire a pastor of congregational life, or pursue a curriculum on the fruit of the Spirit (arguably relevant, but Galatians had not been penned yet). Instead, Paul began by calling them to attend to God's grace and their own stories of being transformed and engaged in God's missional initiatives. When his letter is read, these opening verses should generate an engaging and hopeful community conversation around the experiences he referenced. Do you remember when we first gathered to worship Jesus? Can you recall how the Holy Spirit transformed us, our families, our loyalties? Who can remember how we began to visit our families and friends nearby, how we prayed for their hearing, how joyfully we celebrated new churches? "Can someone give a witness?" These narratives of participation in God's good news, these stories of gratitude, are required if the community is to have wisdom and courage to live into new challenges.

Gratitude, Wisdom, and the Learning Community

Without gratitude, without all the foundational meanings that created and sustained the community, neither the leaders nor the church will know what it needs to know to proceed. Karl Barth wrote, "Grace and gratitude belong together like heaven and earth. Grace evokes gratitude like the voice an echo. Gratitude follows grace like thunder lightning. . . . [W]e are speaking of the grace of the God who is God for [us], and of the gratitude of [humankind] as [our] response to this grace. . . . Radically and basically all sin is simply ingratitude — [human] refusal of the one but necessary thing which is proper to and is required of [those] with whom God has graciously entered into covenant."[15]

The internal and external challenges of an organization need to be

15. Karl Barth, *Church Dogmatics* IV/1 (Edinburgh: T. & T. Clark, 1956), 41-42.

understood and faced in the light of what God has done previously in the organization and in the light of what leaders and participants can learn from earlier (biblical and historical) narratives. Competent interpretive leaders create environments and resources for organizational conversations that generate clarity of meanings and faithful experiments to embody those meanings. Leaders who engender gratitude, who nourish attention to the generative presence and activities of God, will make it more likely that the organization enters into life-giving options.

Leaders who engender gratitude, who nourish attention to the generative presence and activities of God, will make it more likely that the organization enters into life-giving options.

A key responsibility of leaders is to "say thank you."[16] Creative and sustaining knowledge, whether for expected and manageable activities or for the discontinuous and adaptive challenges, must come via the women and men who express their care for the organization and its purposes. Together they can become a "learning community" that lives out a commitment to be continually learning and assisting each other in learning.[17]

For those of us invested in churches and other organizations that are intentional about congruence with Christian faith, our personal and corporate character needs a foundational commitment to the practices of gratitude. In relationships, in our cognitive work, in physical labor, in our uses of time and money, and in our imaginations, we live with full consciousness of God's grace. When we attend to that grace, becoming aware of the narratives and questions and ideas of partners, we are shaped into a learning community that is available to the Spirit's ongoing wisdom. In prayer, we ask. In conversation, we connect and explore. In labors, we manage and create. When these practices are rooted in gratitude, the learning community is most available to the benefits of a growing body of wise leaders.

16. Max De Pree, *Leadership Is an Art* (New York: Dell, 1989), 11.

17. Peter Senge, *The Fifth Discipline: The Art and Practice of the Learning Organization* (New York: Currency Doubleday, 1990) and *The Fifth Discipline Fieldbook* (New York: Currency Doubleday, 1994).

14 Gratitude as Organizational Ethos

Howard Wilson

Editor's Introduction With so many urgent demands upon our time, sincere expressions of gratitude can be few and far between despite all our good intentions. In this chapter Howard Wilson, vice president for student life at Fuller Theological Seminary, describes how gratitude can be built into the ethos of an organization. Gratitude, according to Wilson, is not just an ad hoc phenomenon, but like anything else important to organizational life, must involve a clearly defined process. Wilson, therefore, describes four steps to organizational gratitude: review, recognition, reward, and repeat.

Saying Thank You

The leadership triad we've been considering ends with "saying thank you" — an assignment that initially seems simple but is essential for the ultimate success of the methodology. Without it the leader can become simply a prophet, either trying to lead unwilling people to do something they don't want to do or trying to define a place where they don't want to live. The expression of gratitude for a task well done can make all the difference in a leader's eventual effectiveness. By it the leader integrates his vision into the reality of its accomplishment.

The etymology of the English word "thank you" provides some illumination on the activity of expressing gratitude. The second edition of the *Oxford English Dictionary* says the root of "thank" goes far back in the history of the English language, to around the eighth century. The words "think" and "thank" share the same root, and the first meanings of "thank" appear to be "to think of" and "to think well of." The leader needs to be one who thinks carefully about his organization, and who thinks about the people who are doing the work. Those reflections should direct the leader in expressing gratitude for those who produce the results of the leader's vision.

Without [gratitude] the leader can become simply a prophet, either trying to lead unwilling people to do something they don't want to do or trying to define a place where they don't want to live.

There is an interesting connection between the leadership triad and the continuous improvement process designed by Edwards Deming and perhaps most effectively implemented by Toyota, for whom it is their very essence. Deming's cycle is plan-do-check-adjust, and then repeat the cycle. It requires planning for a process, executing the plan, checking the results, and adjusting the plan to achieve better results. (The cycle in the De Pree philosophy might be expressed as plan-do-check-appreciate.) The leadership at Toyota tracks the continuous improvement process, and plots it visually in a way that all can see its progress and fulfillment. The employees receive regular feedback throughout the process, and at the end of an effective cycle there is a small celebration before the next cycle begins. It is very important to see the leadership approach considered in this volume in the form of a cycle, which results in improved performance of the organization. Expressing thanks to those doing the work reinforces good practices and good effort, and leads to more of the same in the future.

Yet, expressions of thankfulness by leaders to those who work with them are sometimes few and far between. What makes it difficult for leaders to say thank you? There are several reasons why, without thoughtful intent, leaders fail to adequately recognize the ones making the organization successful. By failing to say "thanks," leaders can unwittingly jeopardize their own success and the effectiveness of their enterprise.

First, leaders are often individuals with a high level of internal motivation, with clear goals and a bias toward action. They have a vision of where they want to go and how they want to get there. As a result, they are less likely to seek affirmation from others, and thus less likely to see a need to express it themselves. Good leaders are usually motivated toward accomplishment. What matters to them is moving forward, and making concrete steps toward a goal. If they are systems-oriented, they see a finished task as a building block that, once put in place, does not need further attention. Their thought process may be that of the person who told his spouse, "I told you when I married you that I loved you and when things change, I'll send you a memo." They fail to realize that others may require more regular reinforcement.

Leaders tend to be moving toward the future, rather than reflecting on the past or even actively participating in present activities. Expressing gratitude is a reflection on past performance, rather than on an anticipated future, and so it often gets left behind. Yet, it is often the affirmation of the work done in the present that leads to more success in the future. It builds a foundation for future effort.

Experienced leaders know they are not going to receive many kudos while executing their plan. They have become accustomed to criticism and have little expectation for approval. This doesn't mean that they don't like approbation. They are not averse to cheers from the sidelines and may actually enjoy regular ego reinforcement. However, unlike many, they don't tend to feel a need for regular recognition to move forward. They have the bit in their teeth and are headed toward the horizon.

Leaders of large enterprises often tend to look at their work from the 40,000-foot level — they don't see that those creatures that look like ants down there are actually people engaged in the daily activities of the organization. The leader's eyes are primarily focused on the compass and the horizon, not on the terrain passing below. This can blind her to the impact of the person who has a simple function, yet without whom the organization would be ultimately unsuccessful. In my work I often have to travel, staying in hotels far from home. My impression of a hotel is initially based on the work of three people whose positions are low on the organizational chart but whose work is critical — the person who greets me at the front door, the person who greets me at the front desk, and the person who cleans my room. If this work isn't done well, it doesn't matter what the hotel's bottom line looks like that particular day. The leader of the hotel chain can have a wonderful strategic plan, but if his tactics don't include appreciating the performance of those on the front line, the enterprise may fail.

Huge paychecks for senior leaders in large organizations can also help them forget the contribution of others. When a leader is paid hundreds of times what a person on the production floor is paid, the leader begins to get an unrealistic opinion about his own value in relation to those at the bottom of the corporate ladder. This may be responsible for some of the expressions of hubris and acts of fraud in cases such as Enron. Enron's leaders believed that they truly were "the smartest guys in the room" while at the same time they were ravaging their employees' retirement funds.

Senior leaders have often risen quickly through the ranks of the organization, or have been hired from the outside. They may not have done the humdrum daily activities that keep most organizations functioning. They have little experience or memory of what it takes to shingle a roof on a hot day or enter data into a computer for several hours or stand on their feet at the front counter and serve cantankerous customers for their entire shift. Leaders may not have done much, if any, of that type of work, or their memory may have faded from when they experienced those hours of tedium, and as a result they minimize the importance of it. I am fortunate in that my work history includes time spent as a machinist's helper and a tractor assembler. It helps me to appreciate what it means to do the same task, standing in one place, over and over again, and it reminds me to say thank you to those who do similar things for me now.

Leaders are also hindered in saying thank you because their work life is generally interesting and often highly variable. While their calendars are full to overflowing, they still have a significant amount of control over their lives and get to have new experiences. Their work often includes some travel, though that can become less of a benefit and more of a hindrance as it increases in frequency. This richness in their own experience can blind them to the work life of those who operate the same machine each day, punching holes into a piece of metal. Or those who set up a conference room for a meeting only to have to take down the furniture, clean the room, and set it up yet once again. The leader can forget to thank those who "stand and wait."

An effective leader needs to be intentional about saying "thanks," as it may not be an automatic behavior.

Because of these challenges, an effective leader needs to be intentional about saying "thanks," as it may not be an automatic behavior. It requires thoughtful reflection and careful execution, and is crucial to the success of the enterprise. The leader is the person who inculcates a culture of gratitude into the organization. The organization will only be fully effective if the principle of gratitude for a job well done percolates through the enterprise from top to bottom. Once this has been established, the responsibility of the senior leader is to ensure that the practice continues.

How does a leader develop this culture of gratitude? There are at least four components:

- **Review** — what good things are happening within the organization?
- **Recognition** — how do we bring successful people to the attention of others?
- **Reward** — what do we give to those whose work moves us forward?
- **Repeat** — how do we keep the cycle going?

Review

Saying thank you begins with a time of reflection, a time "to think of" the contribution of those who are being led. This requires the leader to look carefully at the organization, to see who stands out. Which team member is doing something that has led to the success of the enterprise? Who is making a difference? Who do the customers appreciate? The leader needs to pay attention to all levels of the organization, or, if the organization is very large, to be sure that lower-level leaders are also thinking about what their people are doing.

Part of the review process can be built into the routine life of the organization. Regular performance reviews can allow leaders to spend some effective time with those who serve them, and say "thanks" for what they have done. If the performance review involves some small constructive criticism, the leader needs to be careful to emphasize the success, not the weakness. I once worked with a colleague who gave an employee a very favorable review. However, he had one criticism about the individual's punctuality. His tone led her to believe that this was a major problem, and all she heard for the rest of the review was "You don't get to work on time" rather than "You're the best administrative assistant I've ever had."

At my organization we celebrate employees who have reached milestones in their employment — five, ten, fifteen, twenty years and more.

The human resources department keeps accurate records of employment history, and several weeks before the event asks the employee's supervisor to write a paragraph about the contribution the employee has made to the life of the school. These are then gathered into a printed booklet that is distributed at the celebration. It's a great exercise in reflecting on the person and considering what he or she does. And the employees who are recognized treasure that booklet.

One of the simplest ways to regularly say "thank you" is through birthday cards.

One of the simplest ways to regularly say "thank you" is through birthday cards. My assistant keeps a calendar of birthdays for employees in the area I manage. I write a personal note, thanking them for their contribution to our work, and enclose a small gift certificate. I receive dozens of responses from these cards, from people who appreciated the small recognition of their service. Perhaps the most important aspect is maintaining an accurate list, as feelings can be hurt if I miss someone's birthday.

It is very important that the review process be broad-based and equitable. People will react very negatively to perceived favoritism or bias in selecting people to thank. An option is to have a program where other employees can suggest people who have made a particular impact. At the same time, it is also true that not every person should be thanked. Rewarding poor performance communicates the wrong message to the team, and hinders success.

Recognition

The most important aspect of the process is recognition — thanking people for what they have done. The leader needs to be sincere and appreciative of the impact of others.

There are two sides to recognition, public and private, and the leader must use both wisely. The private "thank you" can be very effective. Kenneth Blanchard champions it in *The One Minute Manager.* He recommends short, private one-on-one conversations between the leader and the employee, with a firm handshake and an expression of gratefulness for what the person has done. The private "thank you" can also be communicated in a brief letter or note, expressing gratitude for the recipient's effort. These are sometimes very effective, because the recipient often keeps the message and refers back to it. I received a short typewritten note once from Max De Pree, for a sermon I gave at a board of trustees meeting. I keep it in my desk and will keep it for a long time. It was warm and to the point, and provides reinforcement for those times when the role of leadership seems hard. An e-mailed "thank you" is probably less effective than a handwritten note. E-mail is an ephemeral medium that often doesn't communicate emotions adequately, and it can be transmitted without much control.

Usually the most effective recognition is public recognition. However, the leader must be sensitive to the nature of the person being thanked. Some individuals are so shy that any activity that requires them to stand up in front of people is painful, and the pain can have more impact than the reward. These individuals are few in number, but they need to be handled with grace.

Effective recognition requires the participation of senior leadership, but within reason. The leader should know the person receiving the praise, and that person should be familiar with the leader. Bringing in a CEO to a branch manufacturing plant to hand out awards is sometimes ineffective, because the employee knows that the executive doesn't really know much about his or her contribution, and the effort can seem insincere. The manager who is seen on the shop floor regularly can be a more effective presenter.

The best time to thank someone is while the person is doing the work. Unfortunately, we often wait for some major milestone, like retirement dinners, to tell people how much we appreciate them.

Recognition can be done effectively in large groups. We recently built a large student apartment complex. The project took about eighteen months, and more than one hundred tradesmen were often on the site. At two points during construction we hosted a noontime barbecue, to thank the laborers for their share in making it a great project. Our general contractor, DPR Construction, provided T-shirts for everyone to commemorate the occasion, and some Fuller students and employees joined in the celebration. I gave a short speech, thanking the workers for their efforts to make great homes for students from all over the world. The cost was nominal, but the response was very positive. Many of the workers told me no one had ever thanked them for their job before. Most trades leave a project long before the ribbon-cutting ceremony and never receive any comments from the end user about their work. We saw those T-shirts on the job site for many more weeks.

Recognition needs to be timely. The best time to thank someone is while the person is still on the job. Unfortunately, we often wait for some major milestone, like retirement dinners, to tell people how much we appreciate them. They still appreciate the compliments, but the impact might have been far greater if those compliments had been made years earlier.

The audience for the recognition can be very important. What is often most effective is to recognize people in front of their peers, who know them best. Some individuals may be overly endowed with a pseudo-Calvinist work ethic that says people should be expected to do their best and not seek attention, but generally people like to be honored in front of their friends. Particularly effective is to invite family and friends to the recognition event, especially if the event is a surprise to the honoree.

At the end of our construction projects we have a final celebration, where we honor those partners in the project who have played an important role in making it a success. We have a luncheon and invite donors and contractors and civic officials and staff. We have special plaques made inscribed with people's names and text thanking them for making it a successful project. The plaques are attractive and look like cast bronze, not like something engraved at a local trophy store. The first time we awarded them, my colleagues questioned whether people would really appreciate the plaques. However, the recipients always seem very pleased. When I visit their offices or workshops, I see these plaques hanging on the wall in a prominent place. And the recipients want to work for us again.

Some expressions of gratitude can be programmed into an organization's yearly activities. For example, a few years ago we experienced a good year financially, the result of the entire organization working well together. We had a significant surplus at the end of the year, and we decided to give our employees a $100 gift card for a local department store. Our team leaders handed the cards out personally while people were working, and thanked them for their contribution to our success. We are a nonprofit organization and our employees work for lower wages than they might earn at an employer with a different mission. The gift cards allowed them to purchase something they otherwise might not be able to afford. We have been able to provide the same award in subsequent years, and each year we received dozens of "thank you's" back from our employees.

Recognition can also be initiated by others. We have established a Shining Star award program, which allows people to be nominated by their peers and their managers for making some special contribution to our organization. A committee evaluates the nominations and selects the recipients.

I went to a college two thousand miles from my home and was able to go home only for the Christmas and summer vacations. In my sophomore year my history professor asked me to come to his house for Thanksgiving dinner, and I got to share in a big East Texas feast and be part of their family and forget about how far I was away from home. Twenty years later, when I returned to serve in leadership at my alma mater, I gave a seminar to the faculty on how to make students feel welcome at the school. I used Dr. Ken Durham as an example of what a difference a caring faculty member could make in a student's life — that because of him I had become a lifelong student of history. He was sitting in the back of the room and didn't say anything at the time. Ten years later I returned to the school for a special event, and Ken was still there. I went up to him and told him that he was still one of my favorite professors, and he told me that my comment in that seminar ten years earlier had been one of the nicest things anyone had said to him in his professional career. The size of his smile told me that my simple words years earlier had made a difference for him.

Reward

Saying thank you does not need to be an expensive proposition. Some of the best forms of recognition are the simplest — a sincere compliment, a handwritten note, a comment made at a team meeting. The impact of an appropriate reward can last a long time.

It is possible to say thank you with money. Great work should be recognized by increased compensation if it adds value to the enterprise. However, a raise may not always have a major impact. People's motivation is much more complicated than a dollar sign. Cash gifts often get spent on immediate needs, and may not have a residual effect.

Rewards do not need to be complicated or expensive. Often simple things can be a great way to say "We appreciate what you do." I have found a cigar maker in Tampa who makes fine, hand-rolled cigars. When we reach significant milestones in our construction projects, I distribute them at project meetings amongst the architects and project managers and consultants who smoke. For many of them, it's something they can really enjoy when they relax. And they do like them and look forward to them. Sometimes I see them looking down the conference table to see if this is a "cigar meeting." Even individuals who don't smoke cigars seem glad to receive them. One of our team members doesn't smoke but keeps them carefully in a desk drawer.

The monetary value of the award is much less important than the value the recipient places on it. This requires thoughtfulness on the part of the leader, because "one size definitely does not fit all." A reward can be giving people the resources to do something they really enjoy — tickets to a movie or a baseball game, gift certificates for a dinner out with their spouse, a magazine subscription in a specialty area that captivates their interest. Gifts like that can make a lasting impact.

One special way we like to thank people who have made a major impact on the seminary is to give them a page from a 1611 first edition of the King James Bible. A benefactor gave the school a portion of a 1611 Bible years ago, and for individuals who have been significant in the life of the institution we carefully remove a page and have it framed. These gifts are highly prized, because they symbolize a major part of our mission — the study of the Scriptures.

There are ways organizations can provide a major reward for all their employees. I first became aware of the Lands' End mail-order operation through an article in the late eighties in *Fortune* magazine about firms whose customer service and employee satisfaction were exemplary. While on a business trip I decided to drive through Dodgeville, Wisconsin, to see what their company was really like. They welcomed visitors and were very open about their business model. I went on a tour, and they told me to feel free to talk to employees as the tour wound through their various operations. I asked several employees, "Is this really a great place to work?" and their answer was inevitably yes. One person told me to look across the street at their wellness center for an example of what made Lands' End great for their employees. The tour guide told me that it was a comprehensive fitness facility, with a gym, health club, swimming pool, racquetball courts, and more. The previous Christmas, at their corporate party, the CEO had pointed to the building, which had a huge bow wrapped around it for the day, and told them that it was their Christmas present, as the result of a good year. They and their families were given free access to the facility as long as they worked at Lands' End.

Repeat

The final aspect of saying thank you is repetition — integrating it into the life of the leader. As we saw in the beginning, obstacles arise to prevent leaders from remembering to express gratitude for the work of those that make them successful. Yet, without thankfulness the leader's impact may ultimately be minimized, because he has not made his team feel that they are appreciated, and their loyalty reduced.

The Deming plan-do-check-adjust cycle is always a forward-moving process, building on small successes and turning them into major accomplishments. Toyota has used it effectively to become the largest automobile manufacturer in the world. The leadership triad also moves forward, building on the work of those who implement the leader's vision. Sharing appreciation for the success of the organization as it fulfills the vision makes the team more excited about fulfilling the next stage.

15 Paying Attention to People as Gratitude

Wilbert R. Shenk

Editor's Introduction Gratitude may be both good and wise, but, let's face it, sometimes it sounds a bit old-fashioned. Among a range of human excellencies, gratitude seems to comport all too well with the quaint potluck dinners and the frumpy decor of fellowship halls found in churches from coast to coast. Saying thank you seems about as cutting edge as having a firm handshake and using good telephone manners. In this essay Wilbert Shenk, who teaches theology at the School of Intercultural Studies at Fuller Seminary, challenges this unfair depiction of gratitude by showing it to be an important component of postmodern leadership. Whereas modernity diminishes the importance of humans by divorcing people from their context and by treating humans as resources, postmodern leadership bucks this trend by paying attention to people. And from a theological perspective, paying attention to people necessarily involves being grateful for them.

Every person is decisively shaped by the culture in which he or she has been reared. Each culture has its particular way of valuing the people who constitute its population. It was eye-opening to me when I discovered in the late 1950s in Indonesia that wages paid to day laborers — the ones doing the backbreaking work of unloading heavy sacks of grain or repairing the miserable roads, using picks and shovels — were set on the basis of the amount of food such a man had to eat to have the strength to put in a long day's work. No allowance was made for what he also needed to feed his wife and children. Even though such work was indispensable to society and the economy, in that culture grinding physical labor was socially disdained. Those destined to do such work were relegated to the bottom of the social ladder.

This example from a semitraditional society paints a stark picture. Class structures dictate how people are to be valued. What kinds of rules have guided modern culture? Is work valued more highly in the modern economy than in traditional societies? Modern industrial society has been a powerful magnet drawing large numbers of people from rural areas to urban centers. Social mobility has greatly increased and traditional class structures have gradually become more porous. In response to industrialization and urbanization, where people live, how they earn their livelihood, and the way society is structured have all undergone profound change. Instead of the ordered existence of traditional society, modern industrial society is complex and dynamically changing. And labor is but one factor of production that keeps the assembly line moving in the modern factory. The history of labor unrest, strikes, and the founding of the labor movement in modern society remind us that these changes have been tumultuous. The relations between management and labor have often been adversarial rather than collaborative.

Postmodernity is, in part, a pleading for humane alternatives to the alienation and depersonalization associated with modernity.

In this essay I will explore the premise that "paying attention to people" is not the natural response in modern society. The modern economy is driven by the profit motive, as we are reminded almost daily by corporate executives, economists, and the stock markets. "Paying attention to people" has always required deliberate effort by leadership to manage a company or organization in extraordinary ways. "The laborer is worthy of his hire" means more than paying a fair wage.

Modern scientific culture has achieved brilliant results. Yet its sheer brilliance has blinded us to its limitations. By the late twentieth century postmodernity had emerged as a protest against some of the main features of modernity, especially its corrosive effects on our quality of life as individuals and as a society. Postmodernity is, in part, a pleading for humane alternatives to the alienation and depersonalization associated with modernity. At the heart of this appeal is that we learn once more to value the people around us.

The Power of Modern Culture

Most of the time we take our culture for granted. It is our native habitat. But as Christians we are called to exercise a critical engagement with our culture. We must dig below the surface if we are to understand a culture's inner dynamics and drives. Modernity has been called the most powerful culture in history because of the way it has developed knowledge and harnessed this knowledge to transform all dimensions of human life. Social theorist Anthony Giddens analyzes the dynamism of modernity in terms of three movements.[1]

The Separation of Time and Space

The first movement is the separation of space and time. All premodern cultures had their particular ways of marking time. Time was understood in relation to the space in which a culture was located. Agrarian societies marked time in relation to the growing cycle. For hunting societies time was tied to the seasonal availability of game. In all cases, time and space formed a unity. Each timekeeping system was local, that is, specific to that society.

Modernity revolutionized these two basic elements by separating them. An early step was the invention of mechanical means of measuring time. The clock could be used in any culture to mark the hours of the day. Then the calendar was introduced, establishing a system for keeping time over long periods. Finally, in the nineteenth century a system of international time zones was established that brought the entire globe under a common system of keeping time.

Time and space were now permanently separated. Each could be operationalized as factors of production. Modern industry developed on the basis of the careful measurement of the productivity of each factor of production — raw materials, labor, and capital. Workers were paid on the basis of output measured by the quantity produced in the most efficient manner.

Modern industrial society relativized the importance of space.

1. Anthony Giddens, *The Consequences of Modernity* (Stanford: Stanford University Press, 1990), 16-54.

Workers moved in response to job opportunities. Factories were established in relation to the availability of raw materials and labor.

The Disembedding of Social Systems

The second movement is the "lifting out" or removal of social relations from a local context, on the one hand, and the development of new relationships across great expanses of space, on the other. All transactions in premodern societies had social significance. The marriage of two people was not a contractual relationship between two people, as modern people have come to regard it; rather, marriage was the joining together of extended family systems embedded in the web of the entire community. In traditional cultures bartering for goods in the local market was an important social ritual.

By contrast, modernity devised an abstract system based on bureaucratic principles and procedures that minimized the relational dimension and insisted on following objective procedures. The health care in the United States is one example. By the end of the twentieth century it had been transformed by the HMO industry. Using the principles pioneered by the fast-food chains, popularly called "McDonaldization,"[2] HMOs took over much of the health care in the United States. Every step in the medical care process is anticipated and controlled, including the amount of time a doctor may spend with a patient. The arbiter of the success or failure of health care now is profitability. In 2005 the United States was spending considerably more than any other nation on health care, and yet 45 million people had no health insurance and the overall health of the nation had fallen behind that of other industrial nations.

Various mechanisms have been used to implement this process of disembedding. These mechanisms fall into two groups: *expert systems* and *symbolic tokens*. Modern culture has been built on a wide range of expert systems: airline pilots, dentists, bond brokers, and child-care attendants all have been certified by the appropriate government agency based on a prescribed training program and examination. Modern society puts great trust in this system of expertise. We do not choose experts

2. George Ritzer, *McDonaldization of Society*, rev. ed. (Thousand Oaks, Calif.: Pine Forge Press, 1996). Ritzer's work has stimulated widespread discussion.

on the basis of personal relationship. We first ask: Is this person a qualified expert?

The second mechanism is symbolic tokens. The clearest example of this is money. Over time the form of money has evolved from items that could be exchanged to precious metals and coins, to paper bills, to checks, to credit cards, and now to electronic transfers that entail no physical instrument. Note the progression. Each of these steps has moved further toward the depersonalization of transactions. Paying attention to people is time-consuming. The modern calculus urges that every effort be made to minimize cost.

Inevitably, this pervasive transience takes its toll on human relationships.

Reflexive Ordering and Reordering

Tradition is the great antagonist of modernity. Essential to the modern outlook is the process of continuous critical reflection on an activity in order to evaluate it and propose improvements. Today's solution is tomorrow's problem. Traditional societies honor experience. Wisdom consists of the insights distilled from life experiences. By contrast, modernity values knowledge and information. Modernity rewards innovation. Reflexivity breeds an aura of tentativeness about all knowledge and practice. Our culture drills into us that nothing will last for long; and production processes are based on the continual introduction of new models and products. We take planned obsolescence for granted. Inevitably, this pervasive transience takes its toll on human relationships.

Putting People First

The modern economy is driven by the demand for efficiency, cost-effectiveness, and profitability. All factors of production, including labor, are subject to close scrutiny. The rapid globalization of the economy has expanded the possibilities for industry to achieve greatest cost-effectiveness by relocating. Numerous manufacturers have moved their production "offshore." "Outsourcing" means that corporations are shedding high-cost labor by seeking out low-cost opportunities. The workers now producing these goods in other countries are paid much lower wages and are usually not provided the fringe benefits required in Europe and North America. We cannot depend on the modern economy to put people first. A Christian leader will make people the priority. This will require deliberate and sustained actions that create and maintain a life-giving environment.

A Hospitable Environment

Hospitality is central to the biblical faith tradition. The Old Testament enjoined the people of Israel to practice hospitality.

> You shall not oppress a resident alien; you know the heart of an alien, for you were aliens in the land of Egypt. (Exod. 23:9)

> When an alien resides with you in your land, you shall not oppress the alien. The alien who resides with you shall be to you as the citizen among you; you shall love the alien as yourself, for you were aliens in the land of Egypt: I am the LORD your God. (Lev. 19:33-34)

The people of Israel knew through bitter experience what it meant to be migrant laborers without benefit of civil protection. God instructed the Israelites to treat foreigners the way God would treat them. The New Testament extends this emphasis on hospitality. In presenting the qualifications for leadership in the church, Paul includes hospitality in a list of fourteen qualities a candidate should have (1 Tim. 3:2; cf. Titus 1:8). A leader in the body of Christ must practice hospitality because that is what God has done. Paul exhorted the Romans to "extend hospitality to strangers" (Rom. 12:13).

Paul includes hospitality in a list of fourteen qualities a candidate should have.

Henri Nouwen points out that hospitality is the means by which our hostilities are "converted."[3] Hospitality means creating space for the

3. Henri Nouwen, *Reaching Out: The Three Movements of the Spiritual Life* (New York: Doubleday, 1975), 46.

stranger, making room where someone can feel safe and at home.[4] As we open ourselves to the other, we create relationship where friendship can flourish.

Modernity has subverted hospitality. People from the West are unfailingly impressed when they visit people in other cultures who have not yet lost their traditional folkways. The remark one hears repeatedly from such travelers is how astonished they were at the hospitality rural villagers extended to them. Although painfully poor, these people shared freely what they had. During my childhood in rural Oregon, it was not unusual to have relatives from fifty or one hundred miles away show up on a Saturday afternoon unannounced and stay for the weekend. My mother thought nothing of rearranging bedrooms so the other family could be accommodated and cooking several meals besides. We took delight in these surprise visits. In less than fifty years our culture has changed drastically. Today it is taken for granted that one makes contact in advance. Visitors may stay at a local motel. Meals will likely be eaten at a restaurant. "Hospitality" has been transformed into "entertaining" guests. We receive people in our homes guardedly.

This absence of hospitality is true not only of our homes. Time and space have been stripped of their social content. As a visitor at churches I frequently feel that the "greeters" function as traffic control officers. The main concern is to move people as efficiently as possible into the sanctuary. This is not an environment where people feel they have been noticed and taken seriously.

Can we say that the church is truly the body of Christ if it fails to practice hospitality? If we intend to take people seriously, we will have to cultivate hospitality. As villagers in traditional societies show us, hospitality is not defined in material terms. But in spite of their relative poverty, they share what they have. Hospitality is experienced when we open our lives gladly and share freely with the other. The apostle Paul would say to us: in a culture that has lost its capacity for authentic hospitality, let Christian communities be noted for the way they make room for the stranger.

4. In addition to Nouwen's book, see Christine Pohl, *Making Room: Recovering Hospitality as a Christian Tradition* (Grand Rapids: Eerdmans, 1999), and Jonathan R. Wilson, *Gospel Virtues: Practicing Faith, Hope, and Love in Uncertain Times* (Downers Grove, Ill.: InterVarsity, 1998), chapter 8.

A Supportive Environment

Thomas L. Friedman reports on a visit he made to the Toyota factory in Toyota City, Japan, that was producing Lexus sedans.[5] This factory was turning out 300 cars per day. It took 66 workers and 310 robots to produce these 300 cars. The robots were doing the bulk of the work — hauling materials on trucks and applying rubber seal on the front windshields of the new cars. The humans were present mostly to monitor the quality of the work.

We can read this parable from several angles. The combination of technology and human ingenuity that can produce a high-quality automobile so efficiently is dazzling. The role robots play in performing highly technical operations is impressive. A third angle from which to interpret Friedman's parable is that modern industry is under pressure to continue replacing workers. The question arises: How many workers will be required to produce 300 Lexus sedans ten years from now? The ratio of robots to humans assuredly will continue to shift in favor of the former.

Paying attention to people means creating a supportive environment.

We should not expect the modern economy to be supportive of people. More than 150 years ago Karl Marx exposed the primal antagonism between capital and labor in the modern economy. Without subscribing to Marxism, we can agree that this tension has not disappeared. Labor is simply one factor of production, and it will be replaced as quickly as possible with another factor that is cheaper and cannot talk back.

Paying attention to people means creating a *supportive* environment. This will include three dimensions. First, in a supportive environment the individual feels welcomed and valued. Second, this environment is one in which each member grows as a member of the team. Competence in performing a task is necessary, but this is recognized as enhancing the effectiveness of the team as a whole. Third, our care for others ought to be holistic. The individual is not simply a bundle of expertise. It is demeaning to

5. Thomas L. Friedman, *The Lexus and the Olive Tree* (New York: Farrar, Straus and Giroux, 1999), 26.

be valued only for what one can produce. A holistic understanding takes account of the person and that person's web of relationships: family, religious, civic, and others.

A Challenging Environment

A hospitable and supportive environment is one in which the individual can thrive. A *challenging* environment is one in which people can grow toward their full potential. One of the greatest satisfactions a leader can experience is to see people discover skills and abilities they did not know they had until they were given opportunity and encouragement to try something new.

One of the greatest satisfactions a leader can experience is to see people discover skills and abilities they did not know they had until they were given opportunity and encouragement to try something new.

In the body of Christ leaders should understand their primary role as cooperating with God. Leaders should pay special attention to Paul's teaching on spiritual gifting (1 Cor. 12; cf. Eph. 4:7-16). Paul asserts that all members of the body have been endowed with "grace gifts." The church fails to realize its full potential in direct proportion to its failure to pay attention to this fundamental provision. Effective leadership helps the body stay focused on this essential fact, challenging each member to contribute to the body out of that grace gift God's Spirit has entrusted to each.

16 The Grateful Pastor

Dennis N. Voskuil

Editor's Introduction A recurring question in this volume is how much wisdom from the corporate world can be affirmed and put to use in the pastorate. In this essay Dennis Voskuil, who teaches church history at Western Theological Seminary, asserts that, in addition to being an expedient practice, gratitude is a key theological foundation for pastoral ministry. Gratitude is one of the ways that we recognize and communicate the theological reality of God's active presence in our congregation and in the lives of our congregants. Voskuil not only affirms gratitude as a key to maintaining theological integrity, but he also challenges pastors to take the lead in modeling gratitude for their congregations.

When Max De Pree identified "saying thanks" as one of the essential tasks of leadership, he was not specifically targeting leaders of the church. Having served as the chief executive officer of a major corporation, and as the chair of governing boards of educational institutions, he was interested in enhancing the effectiveness of a wide spectrum of leaders — corporate, academic, community, as well as religious. However, because he was nurtured in a devout Christian home in which the Bible was studied and honored, and has been deeply invested in the life of the church, it should not surprise us that each of the tasks of leadership reflects the core of the Christian faith, and that they are particularly fitting for pastoral leadership.

The Theological Meaning of Gratitude

What does it mean for leaders to say thank you? On one level, of course, expressions of gratitude reflect good manners. Like many of you, I was taught as a child to say thank you when I was rendered a gift or a service. Again and again my parents drilled into me that it was polite to say thank you.

Surely it is important to be polite, but I'm certain that my parents also taught me to say thank you because they had come to learn that expressions of gratitude were prudential. Those who are polite will engender affirmation and appreciation over time. My father often advised me to treat others with fairness and generosity because, in the long run, fairness and generosity would be returned.

Gratitude is a way of life, a disposition, an attitude, a response to the grace of God revealed through Jesus Christ.

Saying thank you may be polite and prudential, but for Christians it carries a much deeper meaning. Gratitude is a way of life, a disposition, an attitude, a response to the grace of God revealed through Jesus Christ. While numerous passages in Scripture indicate that thankfulness is the essential response of those who have been transformed by the gospel, I am particularly drawn to the apostle Paul's exposition in the second chapter of his letter to the Ephesians. Here he reminds his readers that they were born "dead through the trespasses and sins" in which they once lived (vv. 1-2), but that God "who is rich in mercy . . . made [them] alive together with Christ" (vv. 4-5). The apostle then underscores the point that from beginning to end our salvation is the work of God. "For by grace you have been saved through faith, and this is not your own doing; it is the gift of God — not the result of works, so that no one may boast" (vv. 8-9). Having made such an unequivocal statement about divine initiative, he anticipates and answers the concern that good deeds count for nothing. "For we are what [God] has made us, created in Christ Jesus for good works, which God prepared beforehand to be our way of life" (v. 10).

The Reformed theological tradition in which I have been nurtured has been informed by a sixteenth-century confession of faith, the Heidelberg Catechism, which essentially employs the first ten verses of Ephesians 2 as a template for understanding the gospel. The Catechism is divided into three theological movements: guilt, grace, and gratitude. Very simply put, the life of a Christian is to be understood as a joyful expression of gratitude. Our very lives are thank yous to God for grace we have received through Jesus Christ.

Grateful Leaders

What are the implications of this basic response to the gospel — this attitude of gratitude — for pastoral leaders? As Rich Mouw and Mark Lau Branson point out in their chapters, grateful leaders acknowledge their dependence upon God. If we truly live as if we are fully dependent upon God's grace, we will recognize that God was at work nurturing and transforming individuals, institutions, and communities long before we assumed positions of leadership. Branson even suggests that the primary work of pastoral leaders is to help congregations attend to the narratives of God's initiatives and the current initiatives of the Holy Spirit. Since God has provided what is needed for a church to be faithful, a leader should take a stance of "grateful awareness."

At another level, grateful leaders recognize that the very qualities of leadership that they possess are gifts of God provided for the enhancement of the mission of the church. In a culture that glorifies individual gifts and achievements, it is very difficult, even for pastors, to acknowledge that these wonderful gifts such as inspiration, persuasion, influence, and vision belong to God and are to be exercised not for personal achievement and glory but to enhance the community of faith.

It is important for pastoral leaders to constantly nurture and deepen this awareness of dependence. Every graduate from seminary who has been called to pastoral ministry has been advised by veterans of congregational leadership that it is essential to develop regular patterns of personal prayer and study. Yet how few of us actually heed this good advice? Most of us are so eager to do the work of ministry that we neglect our relationship with God — the source of energy and vision for ministry.

I confess that my life of prayer has suffered because of misplaced priorities. When I was appointed president of Western Theological Seminary, I was fully aware that this was a daunting responsibility and that my leadership was dependent upon God's power and grace. On the very first day in my new office I posted the five *P*s above my desk as a reminder of my dependence upon God: prayer, perspective, persistence, play, and prayer (again!). I would begin my mornings with prayer, Scripture reading, and reflection. As the demands of the presidency increased and as I scheduled meetings one on top of another, my time for prayer was squeezed out. And I was a Christian leader whose well ran dry. In the busyness of leadership my priorities became skewed. This is one of the perennial pitfalls of pastoral ministry.

One of the most respected interim pastors in my denomination tells the story of his leadership crisis. This pastor had graduated from seminary with all the requisite gifts for success in pastoral ministry — empathy, clarity, vision, communication skills, and a strong work ethic. However, while serving his second congregation he crashed and burned. Convinced that he was indispensable, that the very survival of the congregation depended upon his leadership, this pastor became caught up in a whirlwind of activities. While declaring dependence upon God's grace, this pastor had assumed the role of savior. Without a healthy ongoing devotional life this pastor burned out. Later, after coming to terms with an awareness of gratitude, he assisted countless other church leaders in keeping their priorities straight.

Pastoral thankfulness is rooted in an acknowledgment that we are dependent upon God's grace. But gratitude has a horizontal as well as a vertical dimension. Grateful pastors recognize that they are dependent upon those they are called to lead.

In his chapter Wilbert Shenk reminds us that we are part of a culture that undervalues human relationships. In an industrialized and information-driven society, we have come to prize efficiency, profitability, expertise, and knowledge and information at the expense of the people around us. Shenk points out that this devaluation of relationships is inimical to the gospel.

We must confess that, even in the church, we often undervalue people and treat them as a means to our ends. Perhaps this is especially true today when struggling congregations seem desperate for transformation leaders, for change agents who will turn congregations around. During difficult times it is so tempting to seek entrepreneurial leaders, ecclesiastical CEOs, who will take the reins of the church and tell us what we must do to survive and thrive.

In his powerfully disturbing little book on Christian leaders, *In the Name of Jesus,* Henri Nouwen warns us about the temptations of power and glory and Lone Rangerism. He reminds us that Jesus modeled a much different sort of leadership — that of dependence upon others. Nouwen tells the story of his own encounter with L'Arche, a Catholic community of mentally challenged people in Montreal. Nouwen confesses that it took him a long time to realize the extent to which his leadership was still "a desire to control complex situations, confused emotions, and anxious minds." But with the assistance of others in the community, he began to get back "in touch with the mystery, that leadership, for a large part, means to be led."[1]

As leaders, we must nurture a disposition of dependence, which results in expressions of gratitude. Considering the fact that thankfulness is central to the gospel, I am always disappointed that so few church leaders are good at saying thank you. Psychological tests of those who enter seminary reveal that most seminary students (and their professors, by the way) have a high need to love and be loved. We are high on the scale of narcissism. We cherish the limelight. Perhaps it is difficult for us to say thank you because we do not wish to share the limelight.

The American church today desperately needs more effective staff leaders who are disposed to say thank you. How often during worship do senior or lead pastors publicly affirm or thank other members of the staff. It seems to me that few staff leaders have learned how to be led, to express their dependence upon others.

In her book *A Team of Rivals,* Doris Kearns Goodwin notes that President Abraham Lincoln possessed an uncanny ability to be led by members of his cabinet. Following his election in 1860, Lincoln appointed several of the key rivals for the Republican nomination for the presidency as key members of his administration because he considered them capable servants of the nation during a time of sectional crisis. Even when these men opposed Lincoln privately and publicly, Lincoln consistently expressed gratitude for their contributions to his administration. Concerned about the interests of the nation, Lincoln demonstrated humility and magnanimity toward the members of his cabinet. Goodwin concludes that Lincoln's willingness to be led was not a sign of weakness but of strength of character.[2]

1. Henri J. M. Nouwen, *In the Name of Jesus: Reflections on Christian Leadership* (New York: Crossroad, 1989), 56-57.

2. Doris Kearns Goodwin, *A Team of Rivals: The Political Genius of Abraham Lincoln* (New York: Simon and Schuster, 2005), for example, see xv-xix, 700-701.

If members of congregations seem to undervalue and underappreciate staff members, it is probably a sign that staff leaders have not learned to say thank you. Healthy staff relationships are engendered by mutual appreciation and affection. If staff members are to be held accountable for their ministries by staff leaders — and this is appropriate — they must also receive private and public appreciation for their areas of leadership. A healthy and effective staff operates in an atmosphere of mutual dependence.

What is true for members of a church staff, who are generally remunerated for their ministries, is certainly true for members of the congregation who volunteer their time and talents to affect the life and mission of the church. It is disturbing, then, that these volunteers so often report that they have not been affirmed and appreciated by congregational leaders.

In his book *Clergy and Laity Burnout,* William Willimon reports that the pastors most successful at engaging laity in ministries of congregations are "those who apply generous and regular doses of praise and affirmation." Willimon recalls a conversation he had with his choir director and some of the members of the choir. They expressed a great deal of frustration because no one in the congregation seemed to appreciate how many hours of work they put into five minutes of music on a Sunday morning. As he listened to these concerns, he not only expressed appreciation for their musical labors but also suggested that church musicians and pastors often shared a feeling of being underappreciated. But Willimon concluded that the pastor must take the lead in expressing gratitude.[3]

The pastor must take the lead in expressing gratitude.

One of my friends in ministry tells about a dedicated member of his congregation who year after year produced a high-quality monthly newsletter that included items about members of the church. One day the editor of the newsletter came to the pastor and told him that she was going to give up the editorship. "Why?" asked the pastor. "You do such a wonderful job of editing." Her response: "Not one person in the church has said one word to me about the newsletter over the years."

Especially in the church, the very body of Christ, of which each

3. William H. Willimon, *Clergy and Laity Burnout* (Nashville: Abingdon, 1989), 83.

member is valued and honored, we must do a better job of saying thank you. Toward that end Willimon made it a practice each Christmas to write letters of appreciation to all the officers of his congregation. In these letters he took time to detail the specific reasons why he was grateful for their ministries. Through their responses to those notes of gratitude, Willimon has learned, to his amazement, how few church members have received thanks in any form for their ministries in the church.[4]

Since becoming aware that saying thank you is an essential task of a leader, I have regularly sent birthday cards to members of my faculty and staff that include words of appreciation for their faithful contributions to the life and ministry of the seminary. My wife and I have also invited students, faculty, and staff to dine with us on a regular basis. Such occasions provide opportunities to "say thanks" in very specific and personal terms.

In all of this, of course, those of us who are leaders seek and need affirmation and appreciation. Despite the clarity of our calls to ministry, it is very difficult to sustain them without genuine expressions of gratitude. We crave affirmation because ministry can be a demanding and discouraging vocation. Because those of us who are called to pastoral ministry tend to be rather sensitive and vulnerable, we can be devastated by criticism or what we perceive to be criticism. As I read a summary of my pastor son's yearly review, I noted all the positive feedback. What he cited, however, were a few sensitively stated concerns. In this context, even a small expression of appreciation will help to lift us up and keep us going.

Even a small expression of appreciation will help to lift us up and keep us going.

Some congregations are very stingy with praise or thanksgiving. And influenced by corporate leaders, they may express their affirmation in monetary forms. Following my first year of ministry with a particular congregation, the governing board wanted to express appreciation but apologized that the tight budget meant that I would not receive a meaningful raise. When I indicated that I appreciated the budget concerns and that words of appreciation would suffice, they were surprised.

4. Willimon, *Clergy and Laity Burnout,* 83-84.

Conclusion

A grateful pastor is fully aware of dependence upon God. Gratitude, after all, is a response to God's grace. Moreover, a grateful pastor is aware of dependence on members of the congregation and the church staff. Living in the light of God's grace and the ability to be led by those we lead will sustain us in our lives and in our ministries. Indeed, one of the essential tasks of a leader is to say thank you.

Continuing the Conversation

17 The Formation of Future Leading Servants

Robert Banks

Editor's Introduction Is pastoral leadership formed only in the context of pastoral ministry, or can this can happen in other settings as well? In this chapter Robert Banks, an adjunct professor at Macquarie University in Sydney, Australia, contends that leaders can also be formed in a number of neglected contexts. Banks examines the family meal, secular community groups, Christian communities, as well as forums with specialists in other fields as important settings for learning about leadership.

We hear a lot about the role of skills-based training, individual or group mentoring, 360-degree feedback programs, intensive simulation exercises, and leadership seminars and courses. While I do not ignore their value in forming leaders, they are not the only or necessarily the best ways of achieving this.[1] Too often there is a focus on these at the expense of other possibilities. In what follows I wish to talk about four of the latter. There are several reasons they are neglected. They are seen as too elementary because of their connection with ongoing family life; as too ordinary because of their association with leisure rather than serious activities; as too marginal to the way group life in churches is organized; and as too irrelevant to the professional development of those in positions of responsibility. I believe their neglect to be a serious error of judgment and would like to see each of them restored to its proper place.

1. A description of a number of these may be found in C. D. McCauley, R. S. Moxley, and E. van Velsor, eds., *The Center for Creative Leadership Handbook of Leadership Development* (San Francisco: Jossey-Bass, 1998), especially parts 1 and 2.

The examples I give below are relevant across the whole life course of potential or current leaders. However, I present them in a sequence that starts with what we can best provide for children who might be prospective leaders. Next I focus on one highly effective way of helping young adults discover whether and how they can become leaders in serving others. Then I talk about a setting that can have profound effects on those who are developing as leaders. Finally I suggest an unusual way in which people in senior positions can further their leadership abilities. As you will note, the examples I give come in turn from the nuclear family, the wider community, the local church, and the workplace. But before going further, I need to comment briefly on how I understand leadership itself.

Placing Leadership in Perspective

I begin with a cautionary story. At the start of a new academic year I fell into conversation with a new middle-aged student and asked him why he had come to study there. He replied: "I am called to be a leader and I have come here to learn how to become one." I was rather taken aback by his high degree of self-assurance and even more by his identifying leadership itself as a calling. C. S. Lewis was fond of saying that one of the main troubles human beings have vis-à-vis God is to think we are nouns whereas in fact we are only adjectives. In other words, we turn what is secondary into what is primary and so mistake a by-product of something for the thing itself.[2] We do this in various areas of life. For example, too many people make happiness their main goal and fail to see that it comes as a consequence of the quality of our relationships, activities, and experiences. To focus directly upon happiness is to miss out on the real thing.

Leadership is less a thing in itself than a function of other things, namely, the kind of person we are, the quality of the service or ministry we undertake, and the manner in which we carry it out.

The same applies to leadership. Despite its grammatical status as a

2. For Lewis's general approach to human nature, see W. L. White, *The Image of Man in C. S. Lewis* (Nashville: Abingdon, 1969), 119-39.

noun, it is actually more adjectival in character. Leadership is less a thing in itself than a function of other things, namely, the kind of person we are, the quality of the service or ministry we undertake, and the manner in which we carry it out. It has to do less with particular skills, techniques, and decisions than with behaving, deciding, and performing in ways that reflect fundamental attitudes, motives, and dispositions. This is why even the language of "servant leadership" is suspect.[3] It continues to place the emphasis on leadership as a noun rather than as an adjective, with "servant" as the qualifier rather than the other way around. It would be more true to the New Testament to talk about our need for "leading servants" rather than for "servant leaders."[4] The word "leader" hardly appears, whereas the word "servant" comes before us numerous times. When people are described as joining with or following after someone, it is as a consequence of that person's character, approach, and spirit more than any specific kinds of abilities, skills, or charisma.[5] When this kind of leadership comes our way, it tends to possess a number of common features, among them the three that form the organizing structure for this volume — defining reality, being servants, and exhibiting thankfulness.

3. See, inter alios, Robert K. Greenleaf, *Servant Leadership: A Journey into the Nature of Legitimate Power and Greatness* (New York: Paulist, 1977); L. C. Spears, ed., *Reflections on Leadership: How Robert K. Greenleaf's Theory of Servant Leadership Influenced Today's Top Management Thinkers* (New York: Wiley, 1995); Spears, ed., *Insights on Leadership: Service, Stewardship, Spirit, and Servant-Leadership* (New York: Wiley, 1998); and, from my own country, L. McInnes-Smith, "Servant Leadership: Living a Life Worth Following," in *Lessons in Leadership: Insights into Business from Ten of Australia's Leading Consultants* (Adelaide: 21st Century Success Publications, 2002). There is a critique of some weaknesses in the idea in S. Roels, *Moving beyond Servant Leadership* (Pasadena, Calif.: De Pree Leadership Center, 1999).

4. For more on this see R. Banks and B. Ledbetter, *Reviewing Leadership: A Christian Evaluation of Current Approaches* (Grand Rapids: Baker Academic, 2004), 107-11, 133-35, and compare Siang-Yang Tan, *Full Service: Moving from Self-Serve Christianity to Total Servanthood* (Grand Rapids: Baker, 2006), and his article earlier in this volume.

5. The biblical basis for what I am saying here is explored further in *Reviewing Leadership*, 35-42, and, in more detail, in my *Paul's Idea of Community* (Peabody, Mass.: Hendrickson, 1994), 139-58, 170-88.

Robert Banks

Neglected Contexts in Forming Leaders

Revitalizing Basic Elements of Family Life

Two brothers who became major leaders in their denomination were asked about their early preparation for their present roles. This began, they said, with their mother telling them from a very early age that one day they would lead others and with her encouraging them to take charge of whatever activities they were involved in. I was troubled by their response, partly because this seemed a questionable goal to place before young children and partly because I have not always felt comfortable with the way they have exercised leadership. Far more in keeping with a Christian approach would be to ask how we can best provide children with opportunities to develop a sense of assisting others rather than controlling them. This would begin with looking at how children can learn to serve others through undertaking regular chores and responsibilities in the family and being on the lookout for ways of helping others in the neighborhood and school. I could say more about this, but since I identify the ability to define reality as basic to serving others, let me instead consider the most effective context for nurturing this among children. How much do we help them grasp what is really going on in, through, and beneath all their experiences? In my experience most families do very little in this area, at least intentionally. When parents and children talk about such things, mostly it is at a surface level. What goes on at school or at church, in sport or on the street, among relatives and among friends — even within the family — revolves mostly around sharing news and gossip, making superficial judgments and interpretations, and expressing conventional attitudes and reactions. Too often we fail to help family members discern the range of hidden agendas and curriculums, unconscious drives and expectations, and gender and power conflicts that affect so much of what happens.

The best time and place for them to learn how to pass all they are involved in through a reality check appropriate to their age is regular conversations around the dinner table.[6] Unfortunately shared meals —

6. On the general but largely underrated importance of conversation, see my article on the subject in Robert Banks and Paul Stevens, eds., *The Complete Book of Everyday Christianity: An A-Z Guide on Following Christ in Every Aspect of Life* (Grand Rapids: Eerdmans, 1997), 231-35.

where the whole family catches up with each other, the day's events, what's happening in the world, and where God is in the midst of all this — happen less and less frequently. They also miss out on interaction with specially invited dinner guests who offer perceptive insights on various aspects of life. A different two brothers to those I mentioned earlier, who are well-known national leaders in my own country, attribute their range of interests, development of their views, and capacity to articulate them precisely to such conversations around the family table while they were growing up.[7] Unless we reclaim this basic context for developing our children's ability to define reality, they will not acquire enough of a basic prerequisite for developing leadership. Of course, such conversations will be of limited value if children are restricted from a wide and vital exposure to life around them. All too often today — out of an exaggerated fear of secularism, the priority given to tangible success and achievement, and a near obsession with safety — we unduly narrow their range of experiences, relationships, and involvements, encouraging them to mix mainly with others like themselves in relatively risk-free environments. The result is that they lack sufficiently broad and deep experience of reality itself. It remains only to mention that as children grow older, the family meal needs to be supplemented and ultimately replaced by conversations around the table with friends and colleagues that have the same honest, open, and reality-searching character.[8]

Getting Involved in a Secular Interest Group

Several years ago the well-known American evangelist Leighton Ford spoke to a group of students, administrators, and faculty on differences between past and future leadership. Among other things, he noted how little the coming generation of leaders would be able to depend on cleri-

7. I am referring to Tim and Peter Costello, the former, head of World Vision Australia, and the latter, deputy leader of the Federal Liberal Party. Some reference to what is described above can be found in Tim Costello's *Streets of Hope: Finding God in St. Kilda* (Sydney: Allen and Unwin and Albatross Press, 1998), 29ff.

8. A fascinating treatment of the value of these kinds of contexts for a wide range of purposes is in R. Oldenburg, *The Great Good Place: Cafés, Coffee Shops, Community Centers, Beauty Parlors, General Stores, Bars, Hangouts, and How They Get You through the Day* (New York: Marlowe and Co., 1989).

cal or professional help to gain acceptance and confidence. They would be able to win these only through the exercise of "informal" rather than "formal" leadership, that is, by acquiring the allegiance of others through the quality of who they were, what they did, and how they went about it.[9] How could students find out whether they possessed these characteristics and put themselves in a position to best develop them? Field experience in a congregation or parachurch was not enough to provide this. Instead, either in addition to or as a temporary alternative of field experience, he suggested joining a group, club, or association that revolved around a personal interest or hobby, e.g., photography, hiking, craft work, singing, collecting, etc. While he did not rule out organizations with a humanitarian or social justice agenda, he felt it was more important to follow a genuine interest than a sense of duty.

In joining such a group, he said, you should give yourself to it in exactly the same way as other members. That is, you should pursue your interest or hobby with the same kind of passion as they did, and through that get to know some members more closely. As you did this, he said, it would gradually become clearer whether you could get along with such people as simply a peer, whether your willingness to serve the organization inclined other members to entrust you with a formal position within it, and whether your passion for what brought members together drew others toward you in mutual projects. This is how you could best discover whether you really had the qualities for becoming leaders in the world or church. In addition, you would learn how effectively you were able to relate to a range of ordinary people and open up the possibility of appropriately sharing the gospel with them.[10] In a later stage of life, belonging to such an interest group could be replaced by representing an organization involved in a multiorganizational ap-

9. The idea of "informal leadership" is discussed extensively by, among others, R. Heifetz, *Leadership without Easy Answers* (Cambridge: Harvard University Press, 1994), especially in his section "Leading without Authority," 183-231.

10. On his general approach to leadership, see Leighton Ford, *Transforming Leadership: Jesus' Way of Creating Vision, Shaping Values, and Empowering Change* (Downers Grove, Ill.: InterVarsity, 1991). Though he does not talk about voluntary associations in particular, Max De Pree has written eloquently about what business leaders may learn from nonprofit organizations, within which volunteers often play a significant role, in his *Leading without Power: Finding Hope in Serving Community* (San Francisco: Jossey-Bass, 1997).

proach to some significant social, racial, or cultural challenge, such as cooperation between businesses, professions, social agencies, civic authorities, and the church. For there again, though on a higher level, emergence as a leading figure in the process arises from the informal recognition gained through the contribution one makes rather than any formal position.

Becoming Committed to a Basic Christian Community

When people think and write about groups for preparing leaders, they tend to have only certain kinds of groups in mind. Within church settings, this often involves a younger person becoming an apprentice to an existing leader in a group focused on a particular interest, such as Bible study or prayer, or activity, such as evangelism or pastoral care. One limitation here is the tendency to major so much on the interest or activity that the relational dimension gets pushed into the background. Another is the way leadership in such groups is often reserved for men. Given the importance of emotional intelligence for effectively working with others, both drawbacks weaken the development of genuine leadership ability.[11] Within workplace settings, group preparation of leaders will often take the form of intensive short-term experiences involving teams engaged in high-risk activities where those who tend to take charge are regarded as the ones most likely to succeed in leadership roles. A limitation here is the difference between what happens during such an intensive experience and the less dramatic, more complex, and long-term reality of ordinary working life. Another is the tendency to draw on more extroverted, stereotyped views of what leadership involves.

Whatever the undeniable secondary value of such groups in the workplace or church, the most basic context for developing a sober estimate of the kind of leadership a person might provide, along with the emotional and relational dimension required for it, is in groups of a different kind. These go under different names, for example a communal or a covenantal or an ecclesial group rather than one focused primarily on a particular interest or activity.

A communal group contains people of varying ages, including

11. Daniel Goleman, *Emotional Intelligence* (New York: Bantam Books, 1995).

children, both genders, and different educational levels or classes. The aim of the group is more holistic than those focused on an interest or activity. This is to develop a common identity and life — through learning together from Scripture what God has to teach them, encouraging and nurturing the gifts and character of all who belong to it, helping each person work out how God is calling that person to serve him in the family, workplace, community, and church, and allowing his or her life to reach out through word and deed to those who do not know God so that eventually the group will grow and multiply.[12] In such a group everyone contributes, though the kind, quality, and frequency of these contributions will vary from one person to another and even for the same person over a period of time. With the help of the Bible, and the input of more mature members, responsibility for how all this takes place is vested in the whole group rather than in a leader. This means that the whole group, through discussion and prayer, makes all basic decisions concerning the group's life, direction, and challenges. As one who has been involved in communal groups for several decades, I am convinced that they provide the best context in which members can find out what their actual gifts are — as opposed to those they would simply like to have or are misguidedly taught are most important. They are also the most basic setting for discerning how all members — women and men, old and young, more educated and less educated — can learn to lead the rest in some manner and on some occasions. In time a few members will gradually begin to stand out for the way they serve others both inside and outside the group in various leading-edge ways.

Participating in Nonspecific Leadership Development

Some time ago I was talking with a group of businesspeople about ways people in highly responsible positions could be more effectively developed as leaders. I told the story of a company whose CEO arranged for his

12. On the history, character, and value of such groups, see the full account in Robert Banks, *The Church Comes Home* (Peabody, Mass.: Hendrickson, 1998), 172-79, and regarding their contribution to understanding and negotiating the realities of everyday life, my *Redeeming the Routines: Bringing Theology to Life* (Grand Rapids: Baker, 1993), 99-103.

senior managers to spend time each month with a series of experts brought in from outside. While this was a substantial investment of time, he felt it time well spent in terms of the company's continued growth. As I spoke, a few heads began to nod around the room, though some people were clearly reserving judgment. I went on to explain that the experts the CEO invited had nothing specifically to do with the day-to-day world of business. The guests came from a wide range of disciplines and were creative thinkers with an ability to communicate their ideas to a wider audience. They were not even drawn primarily from such fields as economics, technology, or communications, but included philosophers, sociologists, and even theologians. As I listed these, the number of heads around the room that had been nodding in agreement noticeably diminished.

Communal groups provide the best context in which members can find out what their actual gifts are — as opposed to those they would simply like to have or are misguidedly taught are most important.

One of those listening raised the obvious objection. "But what would these people know about the complex and hardheaded world of business?" The CEO's reply ran something like this: "I invite such people because they have a demonstrated wisdom in an important field. Since all truth is connected, what is fresh and stimulating in one area will always have a potential relevance to others. Once that is discerned, it will lead to new ideas and vitality in those areas as well. While these guests will not know how to connect their insights and discoveries to the business world, if my senior managers cannot make that connection, then I have appointed the wrong people to those positions." Too often when senior managers in companies — or senior pastors in churches and senior administrators in Christian organizations — get together, they concentrate on ideas relating only to their own structures. (For this reason it was always a great disappointment to me to find that so many seminary faculty, and in one case a seminary president, read only theology.) With some exceptions, courses and programs in leadership studies also tend to focus too narrowly on leadership theory, dynamics, and development at the expense of a wider range of knowledge that could broaden and deepen their understanding of leadership. By the way, the company from which I drew my initial illustration here became one of the most profitable in its field and was regarded as one of the best institutions to work for in America.[13]

Raising a Final Challenge

Because for much of his life Max De Pree involved himself in seminary life, it is appropriate to conclude with a few remarks about the seminary as a context for leadership preparation. In the spirit of Max's belief that a central part of a leader's equipment was the ability to ask good questions, I would like to cast these remarks in that form rather than as recommendations. To return to the story with which I began this article, even if few students would be as up front as the one who said he had enrolled in seminary to become a leader, most graduating students can hardly wait to be in charge of some ministry program within a church or Christian organization or, as quickly as possible, to be running the whole show themselves. This suggests that basically they are more interested in leading than serving, and that a great responsibility lies upon seminary teachers and administrators to model to students what being leading servants really involves. What do those in contact with us pick up from us as we carry out our responsibilities and as we relate to them? Do we come across in our encounters, meetings, offices, and classrooms more as servant leaders, with too much of the whiff of the self-important noun about us, even perhaps as we teach others about ministry or leadership itself? Or do we come across primarily as leading servants who are seeking to excel in serving God and others in ways that will be best for, and best develop the abilities and character in, all?

Too often when senior managers in companies — or senior pastors in churches and senior administrators in Christian organizations — get together, they concentrate on ideas relating only to their own structures.

When I taught at seminary level I helped set up a monthly meeting of younger pastors and parachurch leaders who had been very creative and effective in the ways they went about their ministry. Our goal was to learn

13. If you haven't already guessed the company's name, it was Herman Miller, and its CEO none other than Max De Pree, from whom I learned this in conversation.

from their stories what attitudes, motives, and practices enabled them to become so effective, and then to discern what the seminary could do better in this regard. Particularly striking was the way the members of the group had been galvanized into their current form of ministry by "a hunger for greater reality" in their relationship with God, among fellow church members, and for the impact of their ministry on people's day-to-day lives. In sharing these findings with a cross section of board members, faculty, and student leaders afterward, I suggested that this raised a real challenge. Our efforts to give students as full a knowledge of God and ministry as possible in a limited time tended to result in their feeling satiated at the end of their program. Indeed, they were delighted to be getting away for a time from having to gain any more knowledge. Does this not suggest that there is something wrong with our model of instruction, which places too much emphasis on pouring information into students and too little upon helping them to be inwardly transformed by it, to test it out in practice and then desire to start the process all over again? If one of the marks of the creative leader of the future is a hunger for greater spiritual, relational, and practical reality, how can we reform our educational goals and methods as well as the organization as a whole for that to happen?[14]

14. In a general way, applicable to wider educational structures, there is much to stimulate thinking in this area in Peter B. Vaill, *Spirited Leading and Learning: Process Wisdom for a New Age* (San Francisco: Jossey-Bass, 1998). For seminaries in particular, see Robert Banks, *Reenvisioning Theological Education: Exploring a Missional Alternative to Current Models* (Grand Rapids: Eerdmans, 1999), especially 174-81, 211-17, and 224-40.

18 A Leadership Library for Pastors

Editor's Introduction Since they are ministers of *Word* and sacrament, it should come as no surprise that many pastors tend to have a weakness for books. This explains in part why as we accumulate years of experience in pastoral ministry, our personal libraries tend to grow as well. However, not all the books we pick up along the way serve us equally well. Some become good friends and reliable guides while others do little more than take up valuable real estate on our bookshelves. In my experience, most of the books that have proven to be really useful have been recommended to me by a trusted friend or colleague. In this chapter, Scott Cormode, who teaches leadership development at Fuller Seminary, recommends a few books and articles that he has found to be helpful for teaching pastors about leadership. If one wants to develop a useful library for pastoral leadership, these items would be a good place to start.

Argyris, Chris. "Good Communication That Blocks Learning." *Harvard Business Review,* July-August 1994, 77-85.[1]

Augsburger, David. *Dissident Discipleship.* Grand Rapids: Brazos, 2006.

Banks, Robert, and Bernice M. Ledbetter. *Reviewing Leadership: A Christian Evaluation of Current Approaches.* Grand Rapids: Baker, 2004.

Bass, Richard, ed. *Leadership in Congregations.* Herndon, Va.: Alban Institute, 2007.

Bolman, Lee, and Terrence Deal. *Reframing Organizations.* 3rd ed. San Francisco: Jossey-Bass, 2003.

1. This and other *Harvard Business Review* articles are available online at www.hbsp.harvard.edu.

Branson, Mark Lau. *Memories, Hopes, and Conversations: Appreciative Inquiry and Congregational Change.* Herndon, Md.: Alban Institute, 2004.

Carroll, Jackson. *As One with Authority.* Louisville: Westminster John Knox, 1991.

Chait, Richard, et al. *Governance as Leadership: Reframing the Work of Nonprofit Boards.* Hoboken, N.J.: Wiley, 2005.

Collins, James C. *Good to Great.* San Francisco: HarperBusiness, 2001.

———. *Good to Great and the Social Sectors: A Monograph to Accompany* Good to Great. Jim Collins, 2005.

———. "The Good to Great Pastor: An Interview with Jim Collins." *Leadership Journal,* Spring 2006.

Conger, Jay. *Learning to Lead.* San Francisco: Jossey-Bass, 1992.

Conger, Jay, and Beth Benjamin. *Building Leaders.* San Francisco: Jossey-Bass, 1999.

De Geus, Arie. "Planning as Learning." *Harvard Business Review,* May-April 1988.

De Pree, Max. *Leadership Is an Art.* New York: Dell, 1989.

———. *Leadership Jazz.* New York: Dell, 1992.

———. "Leadership and Moral Purpose." *Hospital Health Services Administration* 39, no. 1 (Spring 1994): 133-38.

———. *Called to Serve: Creating and Nurturing the Effective Volunteer Board.* Grand Rapids: Eerdmans, 2001.

———. *Leading without Power: Finding Hope in Serving Community.* San Francisco: Jossey-Bass. 1997, 2003.

Fisher, Roger, and William Ury. *Getting to YES.* New York: Penguin, 1981.

Ford, Kevin G. *Transforming Church: Bringing Out the Good to Get to Great.* Carol Stream, Ill.: Tyndale House, 2007.

Gerzon, Mark. *Leading through Conflict: How Successful Organizations Transform Differences into Opportunities.* Boston: Harvard Business School Press, 2006.

Gibbs, Eddie. *ChurchNext: Quantum Changes in How We Do Ministry.* Downers Grove, Ill.: InterVarsity, 2000.

———. *LeadershipNext: Changing Leaders in a Changing Culture.* Downers Grove, Ill.: InterVarsity, 2005.

Goleman, Daniel, and Richard Boyatzis. *Primal Leadership.* Boston: Harvard Business School Press, 2002.

Heifetz, Ronald. *Leadership without Easy Answers.* Cambridge: Harvard University Press, 1994.

Heifetz, Ronald, and Marty Linsky. *Leadership on the Line.* Boston: Harvard Business School, 2002.

Keifert, Patrick. *We Are Here Now: A New Missional Era.* Eagle, Idaho: Allelon, 2006.

Klopp, Henry. *The Leadership Playbook.* Grand Rapids: Baker, 2004.

McNeal, Reggie. *The Present Future: Six Tough Questions for the Church.* San Francisco: Jossey-Bass, 2003.

Mullins, Tom. *The Leadership Game.* Nashville: Nelson Business, 2005.

Palus, Charles, and David Horth. *The Leader's Edge: Six Creative Competencies for Navigating Complex Challenges.* San Francisco: Jossey-Bass, 2002.

Peterson, Eugene. *Under the Unpredictable Plant: An Exploration in Vocational Holiness.* Grand Rapids: Eerdmans, 1992.

Roxburgh, Alan J. *The Sky Is Falling!?! Leaders Lost in Transition.* Eagle, Idaho: ACI Publishing, 2005.

Roxburgh, Alan, and Fred Romanuk. *The Missional Leader.* San Francisco: Jossey-Bass, 2006.

Scalise, Charles J. *Bridging the Gap: Connecting What You Learned in Seminary with What You Find in the Congregation.* Nashville: Abingdon, 2003.

Senge, Peter. *The Fifth Discipline: The Art and Practice of the Learning Organization.* New York: Currency Doubleday, 1990.

———. "The Leader's New Work: Building Learning Organizations." *Sloan Management Review,* Fall 1990, 7-23.

———. *The Fifth Discipline Fieldbook.* New York: Currency Doubleday, 1994.

Srivastva, Suresh, and David Cooperrider, eds. *Appreciative Management and Leadership.* Rev. ed. Euclid, Ohio: Williams Custom Publishing, 1999.

Ury, William. *Getting Past NO: Negotiating Your Way from Confrontation to Cooperation.* New York: Bantam Books, 1993.

Van Gelder, Craig. *The Essence of the Church: A Community Created by the Spirit.* Grand Rapids: Baker, 2000.

———, ed. *The Missional Church in Context.* Grand Rapids: Eerdmans, 2007.

Watkins, Jane Magruder, and Barnard Mohr. *Appreciative Inquiry: Change at the Speed of Imagination.* San Francisco: Jossey-Bass/Pfeiffer, 2001.

Whitney, Diana, and Amanda Trosten-Bloom. *The Power of Appreciative Inquiry.* San Francisco: Berrett-Koehler, 2003.

Wright, Walter. *Relational Leadership.* Waynesboro, Ga.: Paternoster Press, 2001.

Wuthnow, Robert. *The Crisis in the Churches.* New York: Oxford University Press, 1997.

Index